MUSHROOMS

A Beginner's Guide to Cultivating and Using Mushrooms

By Tom Gordon

MUSHROOMS

© **Copyright 2019 - All rights reserved.**

The content contained within this book may not be reproduced, duplicated or transmitted without direct written permission from the author or the publisher.

Under no circumstances will any blame or legal responsibility be held against the publisher, or author, for any damages, reparation, or monetary loss due to the information contained within this book. Either directly or indirectly.

Legal Notice:

This book is copyright protected. This book is only for personal use. You cannot amend, distribute, sell, use, quote or paraphrase any part, or the content within this book, without the consent of the author or publisher.

Disclaimer Notice:

Please note the information contained within this document is for educational and entertainment purposes only. All effort has been executed to present accurate, up to date, and reliable, complete information. No warranties of any kind are declared or implied. Readers acknowledge that the author is not engaging in the rendering of legal, financial, medical or professional advice. The content within this book has been derived from various sources. Please consult a licensed professional before attempting any techniques outlined in this book.

MUSHROOMS

By reading this document, the reader agrees that under no circumstances is the author responsible for any losses, direct or indirect, which are incurred as a result of the use of information contained within this document, including, but not limited to, — errors, omissions, or inaccuracies.

MUSHROOMS

Table of Contents

Introduction v

Chapter 1- The Story Of The Mushroom 1

Chapter 2 - Why Choose Mushrooms? 21

Chapter 3 - Mushroom Basics 39

Chapter 4 - Growing Mushrooms 51

Chapter 5 - Ways To Use Mushrooms 76

Chapter 6 - Foraging And Identification 95

Chapter 7 - The Power Of A Medicinal Mushroom . 100

Chapter 8 - Common Mistakes To Avoid When Growing Mushrooms 120

Bonus Chapter - Growing Gourmet Mushrooms For Profit – FAQ 126

Conclusion 132

Mushroom Facts 135

INTRODUCTION

Welcome to the world of mushrooms! This book will provide everything you need to be a prepared steward of cultivating and using mushrooms to the necessity of your own uses. We will cover everything from the health benefits of mushrooms to how to grow them, from the history of mushrooms to the way they are used in modern-day religious ceremonies.

Each of section of the book can be read independently of each other, so feel free to skip around to the information that is most necessary for you.

As a quick summary to help you get started, in Chapter One we'll discover the importance of using mushrooms to grow and cultivate for your own personal usage. We will discuss the health benefits of mushrooms, how to use mushrooms with care and how to make sure you are handling mushrooms that are not poisonous.

In chapter 2, we will quickly walk through the parts of a mushroom and the life cycle of the mushroom for you to have the most preparation possible for when you decide to grow mushrooms for yourself. It is important to have all the jargon down as you become an experienced mushroom farmer so that when you run into problems (believe me, you'll run into plenty), you will be able to handle them by yourself and research using proper terms when necessary. We will also discuss what a mushroom is.

Next, in chapter 3, we'll talk about the most popular mushrooms to grow for yourself, including varieties such as Crimini, Maitake, Portobello, Shiitake, White Button, and Oyster. We will talk through the health benefits of each one, the difficulty in growing each, and what materials you need to start growing them.

We will go into the specifics of growing mushrooms, covering subjects such as soiling, watering, fertilizing, pruning, harvesting, and other topics related to these. This will be heavy on the technical talk, so be sure to read chapter 2 before you read this chapter.

In Chapter 4, we walk through how to use mushrooms most effectively, whether that be in the kitchen, for medicine, added health benefits, religious ceremonies, and more. Lastly, chapter 6 will be where we will talk through the mistakes to avoid while working with mushrooms and other important notes.

In Chapter 5, we look briefly at foraging for mushrooms and how to identify them, along with a list of questions you need to ask yourself about every mushroom you find – that way, you have a good idea of whether they are safe to eat or not.

In Chapter 6, we will dive in-depth into medicinal mushrooms, discussing what they are, and the physiological effects of the mushrooms. Then we look into the impact on individual systems in the human body, such as the endocrine system, the cardiovascular system, and so on. We'll end the chapter by looking at five specific mushrooms and how they can boost your health.

In Chapter 7, we will discuss some of the more common problems you might encounter when cultivating mushrooms, such as not fruiting, spoiling after harvest, and more.

And, as a bonus chapter, I will answer 12 of the most commonly asked questions about growing gourmet mushrooms for profit.

Growing mushrooms is an amazing journey. I hope you enjoy it.

MUSHROOMS

CHAPTER 1

THE STORY OF THE MUSHROOM

No example of the mushroom's impact on the world around us is quite like the fungi that killed an emperor, which changed the face of Europe entirely. Charles VI was the Holy Roman Emperor in Vienna, Austria, from the 1st of October 1685 and died on the 20th of October 1740. On the 10th of October, at the age of 55, he was fighting a nasty cold as he was struggling under ruling a harsh political campaign in a time of possible bankruptcy, as this was nature's way of telling him to take some time to rest instead of pushing himself. An old saying was that to beat a cold, he must eat to regain his strength; he decided to have a bit of his favorite meal - mushrooms stewed in Catalan oil. Somehow the deadly *Amanita phalloides*, also known as the Death Cap Mushroom, ended up in his stew. He survived for ten days but succumbed to his illness eventually.

After his untimely death, Marie Theresa, Archduchess of Austria, had to bear arms to defend her inheritance from the forces of Poland, Saxony, Spain, Prussia, Bavaria, and France. This was known as the Austrian Succession War from 1740 to 1748, and while Maria was able to save her crown, there was still a huge change in Europe. According to some scholars, the instability in Austria seemed to even leak into the War of Jenkin's Ear between the British, Spanish, and the Caribbean, and affected people as far as India; this event affected the Revolutionary War in the Americas. As Voltaire once said: "A dish of mushrooms changed the destiny of Europe."

In the history of food groups, nothing has been so loved and hated at the same time than that of the mushroom. The terms "mycophilia" and "mycophobia" are widely used now to describe these two broad camps of people. Many eastern countries have historically loved the mushroom for its seemingly magical abilities to treat patients from everything from anxiety to cancer, from headaches to gout. At the same time, in western countries, the authors have gone so far as to call the mushroom "the devil's food" by the Roman emperor Nero, or as the philosopher Denis Diderot said about them: "[Mushrooms] are not really good but to be sent back to the dung heap where they are born". No other food group has been called such terrible names, while at the same time being called the "food of the Gods."

The truth of it all is that the mushroom is a healthy and life-bringing organism that is an important part of any diet as well as incredibly necessary in the completion of the carbon and phosphorus cycle. They are nature's number #1 composting agents, and without them, there would be miles and miles of buildups of dead trees in Northern Oregon and elephant dung piles for kilometers in India. They are full of nutrients and health benefits for all sorts of patients, such as reduction of anxiety for mentally-ill patients to having a wonderful number of antioxidants for a healthy immune system. If you don't end up growing mushrooms for yourself, at least do it for your loved ones around you that can benefit from these wonderful fungi.

Over the years, humans have moved from thinking of mushrooms in terms of good and bad and to a way of thinking that is more based on scientific research and inquiry. We have moved on from superstition and old wives' tales and into medical research and culinary ingenuity for the benefit of people's health as well as their taste buds. This does not mean, however, that they are not still used widely in religious and spiritual purposes, specifically in countries such as Tanzania and Mongolia. Mushrooms need to be treated with respect, for in them carry both life and death.

Louis Pasteur: A Quick Bio

Louis Pasteur was never a big drinker himself, but his scientific duties required him to solve problems with French brewing techniques, a skill that has been "brewing" for thousands of years. In 1857, he began his research on yeast under a microscope only to discover that yeast was a living organism. As he started to do experiments on these newfound organisms, he found that the absence of free oxygen caused the yeast to obtain its energy by decomposing substances that contained oxygen. This process is now known as anaerobic respiration or fermentation, which is the breaking down of sugars in grains and converting them into alcohol, CO2, and other beer flavors.

He also found that to keep beer longer, it would need to be heated at a certain temperature for a short period. This is a process we now call pasteurization, which is now used in everything from wines to cheeses, canned foods to syrup.

Benefits

You are thinking of growing your own mushrooms, and I believe that you do not need to be told that it is a good idea, because you obviously already know that. What you want to know is why it is good to do so. Depending on individual studies and their results, mushrooms are, overall, the superheroes of the fungi kingdom. Mushrooms have been shown to inhibit the growth of cancer cells, to help improve the immune system and reduce blood glucose levels in cancer patients, and prolong the lives of different types of patients and kill certain viruses. Mushrooms are also found to be a wonderful resource for potassium, protein, copper, riboflavin, pantothenate, vitamin D, and selenium. They are especially a great source of protein.

For those of you who are attempting to live a vegetarian lifestyle, or at least stay away from meat on certain days, mushrooms have been a meat substitute for hundreds of years because of their high protein content; they are 10-45 percent protein when dried (they are 80% water on average) When monks were going on meat fasts, or when farmstock was at a low amount, people would use mushrooms as a viable substitute for fleshy proteins. Mushrooms are also extremely important as a medicine, as we will talk about more in chapter 4. They are known to be taken as a whole, created into powders, herbal mixtures, teas, and concentrates.

Research by Paul Stamets has led many to switch their belief system to a more positive one when it comes to mushrooms. Paul Stamets and Battelle Laboratories joined up at Bellingham Washington to conduct a series of experiments. They had four piles of dirt that were saturated with diesel and other petroleum waste. They had a control pile, one was treated with enzymes, another was treated with bacteria, and the last one was treated with mushroom mycelium. The mycelium became saturated with the oil and converted the pile into oyster mushrooms. But that's not all. The mushrooms let out spawns of spores, and then that attracted insects, and then that attracted birds that brought seeds, and that completely changed the environment. It became an oasis of vegetation. The PAHs, or Polycyclic Aromatic Hydrocarbons, went from 10,000 PPM to 200 PPM in eight weeks, an astounding figure, to say the least. The mushroom is a gateway into more productive environments and the nurse for hurting ones.

Paul Stamets has also done research on Agarikon Mushrooms, which are found in the old-grown forest, first described by Dioscorides in the 1st century as a treatment against consumption. It grows in the Northwest of the United States and is extremely rare. They were found to be extremely helpful towards poxviruses. The U.S. Defense Department states that any compound with a selectivity index of two or more is considered active, while ten or more is considered to be very active.

After this worked so well against the smallpox viruses, they went for the flu virus. After tests with individual mushrooms, they switched to trying blended concentrations. This allowed them to take the good from all of the mushrooms they had available to see what the new selectivity index would be. They had a selectivity index of 1,000, which is ridiculously high, almost unheard of in this field. This is all to say that mushrooms are amazingly good for you, and choosing to grow them is an extremely good idea.

Mushrooms are also extremely easy to grow. Once small mushrooms called primordia start to pop up in your growing container after a few weeks, it should take less than five days before you have full-grown mushrooms ready to harvest and eat. You will be spending a small amount of money on the substrate as well as the spawn needed to grow them properly, and because mushrooms do not have chloroplasts and are therefore not plants, you do not need to buy a fancy grow light to have them flourish. All they truly need is room temperature and humidity, so spraying them with a bit of water every day will help them grow wonderfully.

General Knowledge of Mushrooms

In this section, we will go through a couple of different sections of information that have to do with mushrooms. This will give you a general overview of different types of mushrooms, the different categories of mushrooms, their characteristics, and more. Refer to this section when you have a quick question about mushrooms and fungi in general. Here is a table of contents for you to find what you need faster:

Zombie Ant Fungus: What is it?

The proper name for this fungus is Ophiocordyceps unilateralis. Alfred Russel Wallace first discovered this pathogenic insect fungus in 1859, and it was most commonly found in tropical rainforest ecosystems. It affects a certain tribe of ants, and it is characterized by the alteration of specific behavior patterns of the ant that is infected, causing the infected hosts to leave their colony and go on the forest floor where the best suitable environment and temperature is for fungal growth to occur. The ant then crawls to a low-hanging leaf and attaches itself to the underside of the leaf where it eventually dies, and the fruit body of the fungus starts to grow out of the skull of the ant. This whole process takes about a week to occur, including the stage where the fungus erupts from the ant's head, and it releases spores to reproduce and infect more ants. This whole process is so devastating to ant colonies that ant drones have been known to carry away infected ants away from the colony in order to not be exposed to fungal spores.

What are different mushroom habitats?

Most fungi are found in very specific places around the world, in specific environments, so naturally, it is important to be able to recognize these main habitats to best identify and find mushrooms to your liking. And while this book is mainly about cultivating and growing your own mushrooms, it follows that it is important to know more about mushrooms in foraging/identification of mushrooms as well to develop a love for mushrooms overall. They are mostly found in woodlands and grasslands, and for the scope of this book, we will focus on common areas, mostly within the United States.

WOODLAND

Many varieties of woodland support different types of fungal life. Many mushrooms prefer acidic peaty soil, with beech or birch trees, as well as pine trees. Mossy pine forests are rich in fungi as well as oak woodlands, so much so that some fungi are found to be growing on chestnuts as well.

GRASSLAND

Although there are many types of grassland, from wheat and barley fields to more industrialized fertilized grasslands, mushrooms are to be found in all of them. The mushrooms in these habitats are directly associated with the grass and droppings of animals that graze there. There are fertilized pastures and unfertilized meadows, in which fertilized pastures are typically grazed on by farm animals, so many mushrooms grow on the dung of farm animals. Unfertilized meadows have many plant and mushroom species that have to compete with other mushrooms to survive in low-nutrient areas.

How do I tell if a mushroom is edible, inedible, or poisonous?

Most poisonous mushrooms look similar to edible ones, so all cultivators and foragers are strongly advised to make sure they are familiar with poisonous types of mushrooms and to be at least able to identify characteristics of poisonous mushrooms. Popular modes of identifying mushrooms include staining tests, observing the texture of the mushroom, smelling the mushroom for any distinctive smells, perhaps tasting a small portion of the mushroom and spitting out quickly after (this is only if you are sure it is not poisonous, and rather have to decide on whether the mushroom is edible or not), and trying out various chemical tests on the mushroom. The best thing is to get yourself a good identification booklet and use it when you gather samples from the field to be **ABSOLUTELY** certain that what you are consuming is an edible mushroom that will not kill you instantly. Have fun!

How to Pick a Mushroom

Most species can be harvested with a knife, shears, or a small saw that can be very helpful for the hardier samples. Do your best to keep the fungi in a closed container so that it does not dry out and so that it is not exposed to oxygen too early in the process of identification. When foraging for mushrooms, here is a shortlist of materials you should bring with you:

1. Flat Basket
2. Knife
3. Tweezers
4. Collection Box
5. Hand Lens
6. Camera with Macro Lens

7. Notepad and Pencils

Most Common Edible North American Mushrooms

The Field Mushroom - This very common mushroom can be found in lawns after a light rainfall and is a close relative to the common white button and portobello mushroom found in stores around the world. It can be found in fields of grass, and its preferred substrate is the ground. It can be seen in the early fall.

Caesar Mushroom - This mushroom mostly grows in hardwood forests with a ground substrate. This mushroom is quite a beautiful sample, being that the cap is a bright red/red-orange variety with a yellow stem. Its spore color is white, and it has an orange-yellow gill color.

Honey Mushroom - This mushroom is unique in that it grows on wood, even sometimes buried wood. It prefers hardwood and conifer forests as well as stumps in residential lawns. It has a clustered growth habit, meaning that it grows together uniquely, originating from one central point. The best way to identify this mushroom is to look for the ring on the stem.

Wood Ears - Also known as a Jew's Ear, this is a wonderful edible found growing on wood in hardwood and conifer trees. This is a jelly mushroom and has a pinkish-brown color to it, a very easy one to identify with no poisonous look-alikes.

Giant Puffballs - There are no look-alikes to the *Calvatia Gifantea*, a fairly unique mushroom, to say the least. They are pure white and are about the size of a basketball or smaller. When eaten, they sort of taste like plain ice cream. They grow on the ground almost anywhere in the US, but specifically in the Midwest.

Common Chanterelle - These mushrooms have a beautiful yellow color to them, like fresh paint on the side of a house. They have false gills not used for the disposal of spores. They prefer to grow on the ground of hardwood forests, specifically under oaks.

Smooth Chanterelle - As opposed to Common Chanterelles, these mushrooms have smooth gills that are not as sharp. These grow in abundance in the fall in North America and are easy to find because of their bright orange-yellow color. Like Common Chanterelles, these grow on the ground in hardwood forests under oaks.

Black Trumpets - This mushroom is found growing on the forest floor near oaks, and most of the time, there is moss nearby. There are no lookalikes to this unique mushroom, being that it is all black, vase-shaped, and it has very thin flesh. These are known as very good edibles, whether it is eaten fresh or dried out. It is also known as the Horn of Plenty.

MUSHROOMS

Brick Tops - These mushrooms are mainly found on the wood of hardwood forests with a gill color of white, gray, and purple varieties. There are not many lookalikes out there, so no problems there. They grow in clusters on hardwood stumps — a very tasty and hardy variety.

Lobster Mushrooms - These mushrooms are actually a sort of parasite on a *Russula* or *Lactarius* species and is usually found in forests. This mushroom is easy to spot by its bright orange-red color, and it also gets its name from its color — a very interesting and edible mushroom.

Pear-Shaped Puffball - This is a smaller variety of puffball that grows on downed trees in a hardwood forest. It is a beautiful variety with its brownish-white skin, a relative of the Giant Puffball we discussed earlier. They usually grow in clusters and are fairly abundant in areas that they are found. These are one of my personal favorites to eat, tasting similar to Giant Puffballs.

The Parasol - This mushroom is found in conifer and hardwood forests alike on the ground with white spores and gills. This is a famous mushroom for certain foragers because of the hearty taste and abundance of the mushroom. This mushroom has brown scales and a double-edged ring on the stem that will sometimes move up and down.

MUSHROOMS

Oysters - These are one of the most common mushrooms out there, and they usually grow on wood in hardwood forests. They have a white color and can be found year-round in the United States. The best way to identify this mushroom is by paying attention to the fact that they grow off the side of the wood in a shelf-style. This mushroom is very easy to cultivate as well. They also have very widely spaced gills, an important factor in identifying them.

Deer Mushroom - Similar to the Oyster mushroom, this mushroom likes to grow on rotten wood. They also appear in the spring, as oyster mushrooms do as well. However, as oyster mushrooms grow in clusters, deer mushrooms grow by themselves. Also, the stem of the mushroom is centered, as the oyster mushroom is not. This mushroom has a very earthy mushroom and soggy when cooked.

Cauliflower Mushrooms - This one's name is an obvious one; it looks like a head of cauliflower. It is mostly white and grows on the ground of hardwood forests around the United States. Anything that looks similar to this one is also a good edible, specifically its brother *Sparassis crispa*.

Morel - This mushroom is well sought out for in the wild because it is not able to be cultivated, a very tasty one at that.

MUSHROOMS

Chicken of The Woods - This mushroom has an interesting color as well as an interesting name. It is a good edible with a very bright orange color, a good example of a non-poisonous colorful mushroom. This is a polypore mushroom in that it does not have gills, but it, in fact, has pores to release its spores. This is one of my personal favorite mushrooms.

Seven Categories of Mushrooms, And Other Information

1. Cultivated Mushrooms

MUSHROOMS

These mushrooms are the ones that are cultivated and grown commercially. Most farmers can use a very cheap way to work on growing mushrooms. We will talk in more depth about this later. You are able to turn wild mushrooms into cultivated mushrooms by the process of propagation, which we will talk about later as well. Always be ready to identify the mushrooms that are grown by other farmers as well, just as a useful second opinion.

2. Wild Mushrooms

Hunters and foragers harvest these mushrooms from the world around them. Wild mushrooms include truffles, morels, and chanterelles. These can only be grown in the wild, and there is no way at this time to grow them commercially. This sort of activity is where it is most important in being able to identify mushrooms well, so consult a guide or someone who knows what they are doing before you eat that mushroom that you found in your backyard. Remember this old saying: "There are old mushroom hunters, and there are brave mushroom hunters. But there are no old, brave mushroom hunters."

3. Medical Mushrooms

These are mushrooms used strictly for medical purposes. This may include anything from simple health benefits like getting enough vitamins in your diet, or it could be as serious as treating Alzheimer's disease and destroying cancer cells. It seems to me that these mushrooms are the most important ones to focus on when thinking about how to grow mushrooms, and with these types of mushrooms, there are the most amount of uses for them. Some fungi have also been known to reduce cholesterol and been used as antibacterial agents. This includes reishi, turkey tail, and Chaga mushrooms.

4. Psychoactive Mushrooms

We will not be focusing too much attention on these mushrooms in the scope of this book, but when used for research and overall health benefits, these mushrooms are extremely helpful for humans and animals alike. Psychoactive mushrooms, which have the ingredient psilocybin in them, have been used to treat Alzheimer's disease, as well as mitigate the effects of depression and anxiety in certain patients. They are extremely helpful when used in inappropriate ways and can be extremely unhelpful and harmful when used in inappropriate ways.

5. Edible Mushrooms

These are obviously mushrooms that are edible and ready to be eaten by human beings. They are used in different diets to obtain specific results desired by the one consuming them, specifically for vitamins and minerals, calories, and macros such as carbs, fats, and proteins.

6. Poisonous Mushrooms

These are obviously poisonous species of mushrooms found in the wild that are not supposed to be eating, and this helps clarify why it is so important to identify mushrooms in the wild positively. Many poisonous species look very similar to edible mushrooms at different parts of their development, so research and buying your own field guide are very important when becoming interested in foraging for your own food in general. The effects of poisonous mushrooms can range from making you very ill, causing damage to your liver, headaches, or even death in some cases. Be careful out there.

7. Useful Mushrooms (For Other Reasons)

These mushrooms are like edible mushrooms and medical mushrooms, but they are used for different purposes by a variety of cultures around the world. They are not meant to be eaten but rather used for other reasons. Most famously, mushrooms can be used for something called bioremediation, which is the act of cleaning up the environment. They are readily available to break down oil and other contaminants and use the vitamins inside of the mushrooms to create even better compost out of the materials. Scientists are always researching how the mushrooms can be used to replace fossil fuels, packaging materials, cleaning products, and even textiles. By the way, the research is going;

MUSHROOMS

mushrooms can be used for a huge amount of different reasons in the near future.

There are four major groups of genera of fungi: Gasteroids, Polypore, Boletes, and Agarics.

- Gasteroids are the ball fungi such as the common puffball

- Polypores are your shelf fungi that dwell in trees with no stipe

- Boletes are your short and stumpy ground-dwelling gilled mushrooms

- Agarics look most like your typical mushroom that houses the death cap mushroom.

… MUSHROOMS

AGARIC HONEY MUSHROOM

CHAPTER 2

WHY CHOOSE MUSHROOMS?

There are many reasons to grow mushrooms. They are better for the environment, they help you have a deeper appreciation of nature, you will save money at the grocery store, it's an overall wonderful activity, and strangely enough, growing mushrooms will make you into an even better person than you are now!

Mushrooms also have health benefits, such as improved heart health, protection against diabetes, Alzheimer's and dementia, cancer, and they can even help with pregnancy.

Why Grow Mushrooms?

To grow a mushroom is to take part in history itself, as we have explored earlier. Think of the importance that mushrooms have played in the history of the world, and how they have changed the face of Europe in the case of Charles VI, and the ideas of countless authors and writers, poets and storytellers over the years. The history of the mushroom is enough to make this an interesting addition to your home garden and a talking piece for the neighbors when they see your growing parcels, while your frantically explain the actual usage of the mushrooms is less psychedelic than otherwise believed. (As an added note, the focus of this book will be on the legal cultivation of mushrooms that are used by law-abiding citizens, as opposed to their other uses that the author of this book does not necessarily agree with.) But don't sell mushrooms short, because they have more benefits to them then you are most likely aware of.

There are many reasons to grow mushrooms. They are better for the environment, they help you have a deeper appreciation of nature, you will save money at the grocery store, it's an overall wonderful activity, and strangely enough, growing mushrooms will make you into an even better person than you are now! These five reasons all have a few more reasons for growing them within the reasons themselves, so there are upwards of about twenty reasons why you should be growing mushrooms, which is a ton more than I bet you thought about when you started reading this book. We will go through these five reasons in this chapter, and throughout reading this book, you will subtly see more and more reasons pop up all over the pages of this book, like mushrooms tend to do in meadow overnight.

It is better for the environment.

As Paul Stamets advocates in his TedTalk (see references), mushrooms could be a huge part of saving the environment from destruction because of human-based affairs. Mushrooms are amazing because they can create food from waste, so they are self-sufficient, they can be used as animal feed, they help build soil, and they are useful in supporting the growth of other crops and get rid of the need of fertilizer. Check out these reasons to help yourself become an even better steward for the environment.

Create Food from Waste

As we learned, mushrooms are some of the best recyclers in nature, and they can break up almost any carbon-based materials that are produced on farms or by small families. Whether you own a farm or are simply a person from the city looking to reduce their ecological footprint, you can use the materials you normally throw away, such as corn cobs, coffee beans, peanut shells, and many other materials to grow mushrooms upon. Imagine a crop that is produced on the waste of other crops. Amazing!

Self Sufficient

There is a sense of pride that comes from producing your own food. It's a feeling that is long lost from a world of delivery food and instant gratification. You will be able to create as many mushrooms as you wish to fit your own personal needs that you have throughout the years. You won't have to rely on anyone else but yourself on how often you get your mushrooms, but instead, you can be the boss of your own future. Later on, in this book, we will discuss how you can make this a reality.

Animal Feed

If you are a farmer, you also probably have some livestock around that require some food to stay in the best shape possible. When mushrooms are first harvested, they are full of protein and many important vitamins that they absorbed from the waste they grew upon. Studies have shown that livestock of all types benefit from eating mushrooms, and have resulted in improvements in health, digestion, and their immune system. Mushrooms are basically a renewable resource that is extremely healthy for you and your animals.

Building Soil

Also known as "spent spawn," most mushroom growers don't use them for much, so it is very easy to get these leftovers for free. These homemade compost piles are full of benefits, such as their amount of nutrients as well as increased water-holding ability. Mushrooms also help produce actual soil as a byproduct of their growing cycle. This is an amazing trait for an organism that can be eaten as well, a truly renewable resource that more people should know about. These fungi are perfect for corporate and casual farmers alike.

Supporting Crops

Certain fungi can improve the health of many different crops, as proven through empirical evidence. Fungi can make phosphorous usable through the digestion of organic matter. This nutrient is not usually used by plants, as the phosphorus cycle usually deals with rocks and clays, so this means many farmers can use less fertilizer and produce an equal amount of food for their effort. This is very helpful and healthy for both the farmer and the crops themselves. Growing mushrooms alongside your other crops could be very healthy for both.

It Helps You Create a Greater Appreciation for Nature

As you start to grow any sort of crop, you will start to appreciate how they grow in their usual environment. This is especially true for mushrooms because of the rapid growth they have once they start to sprout up. Seeing mushrooms in their natural setting with make you stop with awe and see nature how it was meant to be observed just a bit more. As we touch on next, mushrooms are some of the most beautiful and abundant species on the planet, so they are for sure able to give you a greater appreciation for nature itself.

Mushrooms are Beautiful Organisms

Mushrooms are some of the most widely diverse organisms on the planet, and because there are so many species that you can grow on your own, you will never tire of observing these wonderful specimens. Try out several different mushrooms to get the full effect, and try growing them around the house in interesting ways to add some awesome effects and talking points. If you don't believe me, check out this https://www.boredpanda.com/mushroom-photography full of beautiful mushrooms. In your spare time, check out puffballs, *Mycena Chlorphos, Marasmius Haematocephalus, Rhodotus Palamatus,* and *Phallus Indusiatus.* One of these actually glows in the dark. George Weller once wrote to his wife: "Darling, I am writing this to you by the light of five mushrooms."

The Growing Cycle is Beautiful

Mushrooms are unique in that they grow off of the waste of other plants and animals, and the way they do this is even more unique. Once you see your first pile covered in mycelium, you will know what I mean, as it covers it slowly over time with its long, white branches extending over the substrate. You will then start to see Small mushrooms called primordia pop up all around the substrate you have laid down, and within a few days after that, you will have fully grown mushrooms seemingly coming out of thin air. It truly makes sense why people used to think that fairies and lightning storms brought about these unique organisms.

You will Save Grocery Money

If you start growing your own supply of mushrooms, you will never have to go shopping for them again. The supplies needed to grow your own mushrooms are minimal, and the effort it takes is also very small, so deciding to grow your own mushrooms is a wonderful choice economically, and homegrown mushrooms actually taste better than store-bought ones anyways oh, so it's a win-win.

They Taste Better than Store-Bought Mushrooms

Mushrooms growing at your home do not have to travel there; they do not need to be packaged, and they have not passed through the hands of many different people over the course of unknown time. You can easily grow; you are mushrooms organically as well, which will save you from being exposed to any pesticides and fertilizers used by big companies. They taste much better than store-bought mushrooms because you freshly harvest them.

It's Cheaper to Grow Them

As we will discuss later, we will learn about the number of materials used to grow mushrooms and how they are extremely minimal, and the only major cost is buying the actual spawn used to grow the mushrooms. Growing mushrooms is also not a huge time consumer, so this is a wonderful hobby to partake in. You will quickly make your money back from your investment in materials to make mushrooms. Try out Shiitake mushrooms, which yield mushrooms for five years every five weeks after ONE sowing. That is a marvelous return on investment.

Growing Mushrooms is a Wonderful Activity

Growing mushrooms is a very interesting thing to start doing because not too many people are familiar with this idea of growing your own mushrooms. This does not mean, however, that there is not a large community of people that do partake in this activity. Growing your own mushrooms is an opportunity for education an opportunity to meet new people, and a wonderful way to take up a new hobby while helping the environment at the same time.

Another wonderful activity for the mushroom lover is to forage for mushrooms. We will talk later about the importance of good identification, and if you are able to do this, you will be able to enjoy this fantastic sport. Before cultivation happened, humans had to learn how to forage their own food. Since Jean-Jacques Paulet wrote the first book on edible mushrooms and how to identify them, identification books have advanced greatly, so you will be able to partake in this activity. Children used to actually get out of school early to help their parents in the field to survive the winter. Until recent globalization, mushroom foraging was a national pastime. Later on, we will talk about the cultivation of mushrooms, which was first written about by the botanist Pier Antonio Micheli in 1729.

Opportunity for Education

When it comes to growing your own food, it's impossible not to learn something about the process by which the thing is grown. You will learn about the life cycle of a mushroom, the role it has in the environment, and the overall importance of the mushroom in the ecosphere. You will also learn about the different types of mushrooms as well, and this will make for a grade school project for your kids or for the science fair coming up soon.

Meet New People

You will also learn a good deal of new people as you start to ask questions go to Growing workshops and pass on knowledge to younger Minds that are interested in getting into the process of growing your own food/mushrooms. Most people who are interested in this hobby are very friendly and willing to answer tough questions about what to do when first starting out like a mushroom grower.

Fun Hobby

Overall, growing mushrooms is an enjoyable hobby that most people do not partake in. You will learn many new things about mushrooms and their role in the environment, oh, and it will be an amazing pastime that doesn't take up too much of your time. You will get out as much as you put in when it comes to mushroom farming.

Growing Mushrooms will Improve You as a Person

Out of all of these points, mushrooms are just a wonderful thing to get into more, because they taste great, they help with you getting enough of your nutrients, and growing them is honestly just plain fun. As we mentioned earlier, you will get to know other great people that do the same thing as you, and you will learn much about nature itself through growing your own mushrooms, and that alone is going to change you for the better.

MUSHROOMS

They Taste Great

From Puffballs to Portobello, from Shiitake to Oyster, there are plenty of different mushrooms to choose from. We all have our tastes, and by reading this book, it shows that you are interested in mushrooms, and that leads to the fact that you probably have a taste for mushrooms as well. Be sure to try out a few dozen different species before you knock them completely because many different types have different tastes and textures. You never know what a Button mushroom would taste like in comparison to a Jew's Ear mushroom (actual name), from a more solid fungus to a jelly mushroom. This will be your chance to learn about literally hundreds of different fungi over the course of your adventure.

It's Fun

Speaking from my own experience, growing your own anything is a wonderful experience, and the people I was able to interview for this book had nothing but good things to say about growing mushrooms. There is just something so magical about seeing mushrooms pop up from their substrate after a couple of weeks of growing. You see, after you see the primordial mushrooms sprout after a few weeks, you will have fully grown mushrooms. It just goes to show why people used to think that mushrooms were the result of lightning striking the earth in a specific place.

Missing Nutrients

Mushrooms are a wonderful source for fiber, protein, manganese, magnesium, iron, potassium, and many other important nutrients and elements that are wonderful to have in your stomach. They are a great addition to anyone's meal plan, especially when you are not eating meat. Mushrooms can replicate meats so well that vegetarians have been using them for years, and for thousands of years, monks that would fast from meat for a set amount of time would turn to mushrooms for a meat replacement.

Health Benefits of Mushrooms

While the exact health benefits are usually a bit divided between potential health benefits and empirically proven health benefits, most of the potential health benefits come from historically and anecdotal evidence from the East, such as China and Japan. We will focus on both of these types of health benefits. Both are well supported by data and opinions of people that have used mushrooms for their own benefit. They are used by vegans and meat-eaters alike. Overall, mushrooms are widely consumed as low cholesterol and low-calorie health-promoting food that is helpful in many different ways for all sorts of different people. According to a study (see references) on the recent developments in mushrooms as anti-cancer therapeutics, "The chief medicinal uses of mushrooms discovered so far are as antioxidant, anti-diabetic, hypocholesterolemic, anti-tumor, anti-cancer, immunomodulatory, anti-allergic, nephroprotective, and antimicrobial agents." Those are some big words, but we will get into the brass tacks of the situation and see what that all means for you.

In the scope of this section, we will talk about how mushrooms can help against diabetes (type 2 specifically), Alzheimer's, and cancer. There are plenty of reasons to start eating and using mushrooms for medicinal reasons, but these are perhaps the most important reasons. We will then go through the list of different vitamins and compounds in mushrooms that are helpful in each and every person's life, regardless of sex, age, or lifestyle. There is a massive number of different vitamins and antioxidants that will benefit you in many different ways.

Advocate for Heart Health, Protection against Diabetes

Mushrooms have been shown to have certain phytonutrients that can help prevent cells from sticking to vessel walls helping to lower cholesterol. This has been particularly helpful for overweight adults with type 2 diabetes. Mushrooms are a good source of vitamin C, potassium, fiber, and all of these elements have been known to contribute to good cardiovascular health. Current guidelines call for people to consume around

4,700 mg of potassium each day, while only one cup of mushrooms is known to have about 305 milligrams of potassium. This is why mushrooms should be part of your daily meal consumption, only adding to potential helpfulness.

According to study, the sort of fiber that is found in mushrooms may also help lower blood cholesterol. These sorts of fibers are called beta-glucans. Shiitake mushrooms are especially a good source of these nutrients, most notably in the stem of the mushroom. Mushrooms are also a great source of dietary fiber. A cup of raw mushrooms weigh approximately 78 G provides about 2 grams of fiber, and the American guidelines recommend that adults consume about 30 G of dietary fiber everyday fluctuating based on age and sex of the patient. This is helpful as a nutrient in many ways.

This dietary fiber is obviously helpful in managing type 2 diabetes, as well. For those who already have type 2, diabetes fiber has been known to reduce the level of glucose in the patient, a helpful element. Also, consuming a good amount of dietary fiber in your daily diet is known to reduce your risk of developing type 2 diabetes. So, whether you have it already or are worried about getting it, eating dietary fiber, of which mushrooms are a good source, is an overall helpful preventive measure. The International Journal of Medicinal Mushrooms found that a particular type of pink oyster mushrooms Health reduced total cholesterol and something called LDL "bad" cholesterol in certain types of rats. This goes to show that all mushrooms have low cholesterol inhibitors, but certain types of mushrooms are even more helpful in the fight against heart disease and type 2 diabetes.

Alzheimer's Disease and Dementia

Mushrooms are strangely effective at lowering seniors' risk of cognitive problems. A six-year study of over 600 adults over the age of 60 found that when these adults had two portions of mushrooms per day, there was a 50% decrease in the risk of mild cognitive impairment. A portion was about 150 grams of mushrooms or ¾ of a cup. In some cases, even one portion of cooked mushrooms would have a positive effect on the cognitive decline of elders. Mild cognitive impairment symptoms include not being able to do moderately easy tasks such as cooking a meal for brushing your teeth in the morning. Most doctors see this as the first signs of Alzheimer's, as half of these kinds of impairments lead to developing the disease later on in the patient's life. This study used a white button, shiitake, oyster, and golden mushrooms in their study. ET, or Ergothioneine, is the compound that is found naturally in mushrooms, but not naturally synthesized in humans, so obtaining this compound through their dietary sources is the most successful way to have this compound.

Protection Against Cancer

Multiple varieties of mushrooms have been shown to be able to protect against cancer by inhibiting tumor formation, the same way it prevents Alzheimer's in a more physical sense. This will help against DNA damage because of the actions against tumors early on in their development. According to the National Cancer Institute, the kinds of antioxidants found in mushrooms have been found to prevent breast, prostate, lung, and other types of cancer in recent studies. Vitamin D and Choline are both found abundantly in mushrooms of all kinds, and both have been found to prevent or treat most kinds of cancer, although the results may vary from person to person depending on the severity of the cancer of the patient.

According to a study published in the Journal of Experimental Biology and Medicine, after five different mushrooms were tested, of which were crimini, maitake, portabella, oyster, and white button, they found that the mushrooms suppressed breast cancer growth in certain patients in a very significant way. Shiitake mushrooms actually have something called lentinan, which has been known to extend the survival rate of patients when used with chemotherapy.

Lastly, Clinical trials done at the John Hopkins University School of Medicine used psilocybin, the naturally occurring psychedelic compounds found in hundreds of different types of mushrooms, on a number of different patients that were struggling with anxiety, depression, and fear as they were dying of cancer. 80% of patients had an increasing sense of optimism connection with other people and even spiritual experiences because of the drug. This suggests that psilocybin could be beneficial for people who are struggling with depression or PTSD.

Help with Pregnancy

During pregnancy, folic acid (folate) is used by women to promote fetal health, and mushrooms are actually full of this B-9 vitamin. One cup of raw mushrooms contains 16 MCG of folate, while the current guidelines have us consuming around 400 MCG each day.

Nutrient	Amount of nutrient in 1 cup of mushrooms	Recommended daily intake Trusted Source
Energy (calories)	21.1	1,600–3,200
Protein (g)	3.0	46–56
Carbohydrate (g)	3.1, including 1.9 g of sugar	130
Calcium (mg)	2.9	1,000–1,300

MUSHROOMS

Iron (mg)	0.5	8–18
Magnesium (mg)	8.6	310–420
Phosphorus (mg)	82.6	700–1,250
Potassium (mg)	305	4,700
Sodium (mg)	4.8	2,300
Zinc (mg)	0.5	8–11
Copper (mcg)	305	890–900
Selenium (mcg)	8.9	55
Vitamin C (mg)	2.0	65–90
Vitamin D (mg)	0.2	15
Folate (mcg DFE)	16.3	400
Choline (mg)	16.6	400–550
Niacin (mg)	3.5	14–16

Chart from https://www.medicalnewstoday.com/articles/278858.php#nutrition

CHAPTER 3

MUSHROOM BASICS

This section of the book should be very helpful for you in your exploration of mushrooms themselves. There are plenty of things to know about mushrooms, and hopefully, this short guide will give you the resources you need to become a more professional mushroom grower.

What is a Mushroom?

Most people will class a mushroom as a vegetable, but it isn't. Every fruit and every vegetable comes from an edible plant. And each of those plants shares one common characteristic – they all contain chlorophyll. This is used to convert the sunlight that falls on the plants into carbohydrates.

Mushrooms do not have any chlorophyll and cannot photosynthesize; instead, a mushroom will steal the carbohydrates it requires from other plants. Mushrooms are classed as fungi, one of many different species and, because there are so many species, they even have their own kingdom now, "the kingdom of fungi."

Mushroom Ecology

We can divide fungi into three separate categories, based on the relationship they have with other plants:

1. **Saprophytes** – these are found growing on plant roots, fallen leaves, dead wood, and other organic, dead matter. They take minerals and carbon dioxide from this organic matter, and the category includes medicinal and gourmet mushrooms, such as the cremini, white button, oyster, and shiitake.
2. **Parasites** – these are found growing on living plants and trees and extract nutrients from them. Because of this, they are known as "murderers"; when the living matter has died, the saprophytes move in to clean up.
3. **Mycorrhiza** – these form symbiotic relationships with living tree roots, extracting nutrients, and sugars. However, they also help to enlarge the tree root system by giving back essential elements and minerals. This is a problematic category of mushroom to cultivate and are usually only found in the wild. The class contains truffles, chanterelles, and porcini mushrooms.

MUSHROOMS

Mushrooms begin life as white fluff beneath the ground. This is known as mycelium, fungal threads from which the mushrooms sprout. Mushrooms are fruits from bigger fungi that grow beneath the ground.

In nature, mycelium can remain beneath the ground for long periods, not emerging until the conditions are favorable. Those conditions include temperature, humidity, and food sources. When everything is in favor, small buds form, pushing up to find daylight, and a mushroom is born. The small ball is normally white and quickly grows to a proper form. The cap opens, and millions of spores are dropped, picked up by the wind and dropped elsewhere, where they begin the task of forming more mycelium.

Parts of a Mushroom

In preparation for growing your own mushrooms, it is very helpful to know all the parts of the mushroom to understand their anatomy and growth periods. This will make you a more effective and professional grower. You will also have the skills to identify mushrooms much easier if you understand all the parts to the mushroom. These parts include the spores, the stem, gills, mycelium, hyphae, volva, and the cap. Refer back to this section when you are ever confused about mushroom identification guides. Pros made these guides, so be sure to read them carefully; you are able to learn a lot from them.

Spores

The spores are the agents of reproduction for the mushroom. A single mushroom colony is able to produce millions of fungal spores into the biosphere in a single meter of air. They are extremely small compared to regular seeds produced by plants, spores typically being 1/100 of a millimeter long, and are designed specifically for wind transportation. There are many different types of spores, as they vary in size, shape, color, and other variations that aid them in their conquest of different territories around the world. One fungus, the *Coprophilous Fungi* (literally named the "dung-loving fungi), is a type of saprobic fungi that grows specifically on animal dung. *Huitlacoche* is a fungus that only grows on ears of corn(actually considered to be a delicacy among Native Americans and they even used it as a topping for their tortillas after scraping it off the ears of corn the fungi would grow on), and *Inonotus obliquus* is a type that grows on birch trees in colder climates. Each type of spore has a specific goal in its creation, so mycology seeks to understand these distinctions.

Mushrooms are known as an iteroparous organism, meaning that they produce offspring more than once in a lifetime. In fact, the mushrooms should be in their own category because they so blatantly destroy this definition by producing trillion of reproducing cells over their lifetime. Many spores are, in fact, sent out, but many do not survive. This is why you only see a handful of puffballs in a meadow instead of covering the entire field. The spores may be eaten by slugs, springtails, worms, or any other small predators as they attempt to mature into a mushroom that can complete the circle of life. The mushroom also needs to be wary of competition created by its own showering of spores when searching for food to survive on. The mushroom has prepared for this, of course. Most of the resources of the fungi are loaded into the reproduction element of its being to create as many spores as possible to get them to where they need to be.

Stem

This part of the mushroom is simply the part that supports the cap of the mushroom. In mycology, it is also commonly referred to as the stipe. This part of the mushroom is important in three respects, and I will list them now.

First, it is important as an axis to hold up the cap of the mushroom itself, so that the mushroom is able to work as it is supposed to. Without this part of the mushroom, the cap would be resting on the meadow or forest floor so that it would be exposed to more of the elements. Secondly, the stem is considered to be the mediating factor in spore dispersal. The angle at which the cap is pointed will either make it harder or easier to release spores into the wind currents. However, it is important to note that not all mushrooms even have this feature, such as the puffball, smuts, and jelly fungi. Lastly, the stipe is considered to be very important in making a correct identification of a mushroom, counting such characteristics as: the texture of the stipe, the general size and shape, the color of the stipe, whether it has something called a or a universal veil (volva), and whether the stipe extends underground such as with a rhizome.

Gill

Most of the mushrooms you are most likely familiar with are gilled mushrooms. These gills are papery structures that extend off of the cap of the mushroom that has the sole purpose of producing spores. You could say that this is the most important job in the mushroom because, without these spores, there are no mushroom colonies. Attributes such as how the gill is attached to the stem, the color of the gills and the bruising color that is made when they are disturbed, gill spacing (this one is a bit more subjective but still helpful in overall observations), and length can call lead an avid mushroomer to identify what kind of mushroom they are looking at.

Mycelium

This is the vegetative part of a mushroom colony, the mass of branching hyphae, which is discussed after this section. This mechanism of the mushroom helps absorb nutrients from the ground in order for the mushroom colony to create fruiting bodies or the shapes that we are familiar with when it comes to mushrooms. The Mycelium is what is so beneficial when it comes to the health of the forest and aquatic ecosystems for the role they play in the decomposition of plant and animal material. They contribute to the carbon cycle by releasing carbon dioxide back into the atmosphere as they break down materials into usable soil.

This part of the mushroom is also extremely important to consider when growing your own mushrooms because of the grower needing to be aware of the types of nutrients that are needed to grow certain mushrooms you are targeting, as well as assessing the overall health of the mushroom. Mycelium will either look like an aboveground rooting system or a collection of white mass spreading out from the center of the spore bed it has created.

Hypha

Hyphae are the long, branching agents that collectively make up the mycelium. Think of a tree as mycelium and the individual branches as hyphae. These branches are the main proponent for vegetative growth for mushroom or overall fungi. They spread over pockets of nutrients, and then continue to spread to find more pockets, never being satisfied with their lot.

Volva

This is the remnant of an egg-like, cup-shape part of the peridium of a mushroom that enclosed the immature fruiting body of many fungi. Its most important feature is it's helpful in the identification of poisonous and non-poisonous mushrooms, given that many poisonous mushrooms are contained within a family that has this feature. The Volva is usually completely or partially buried underground, so be warned all potential foragers. Identification guides will take special notice of this part of the mushroom.

Cap

This is the most important in identifying what kind of mushroom you are dealing with. Its main goal is in the protection of the gills and spores just below it, acting as a wall between the outside world and the spores before the stem twists in such a way as to allow the millions of spores to travel to where they need to go.

Species	Fresh weight (x 1,000 t)				Increase %
	1986		1997		
Agaricus bisporus	1,227	(56.2%)	1,956	(31.8%)	59.4
Lentinula edodes	314	(14.4%)	1,564	(25.4%)	398.1
Pleurotus spp.	169	(7.7%)	876	(14.2%)	418.3
Auricularia spp.	119	(5.5%)	485	(7.9%)	307.6

Volvariella volvacea	178	(8.2%)	181	(3.0%)	1.7
Flammulina velutipes	100	(4.6%)	285	(4.6%)	130.0
Tremella fuciformis	40	(1.8%)	130	(2.1%)	225.0
Hypsizygus marmoreus	-	-	74	(1.2%)	-
Pholiota nameko	25	(1.1%)	56	(0.9%)	124.0
Grifola frondosa	-	-	33	(0.5%)	-
Others	10	(0.5%)	518	(8.4%)	5,080.0
Total	2,182	(100.0%)	6,158	(100.0%)	182.2

Adapted from Penn State.

Life Cycle of Mushrooms

The life cycle of the mushrooms remains mostly invisible for most of us, but not with cultivators. If you are getting into growing mushrooms, then you will be shocked at how much you are going to learn when it comes to the overall life of a mushroom. By knowing all the parts to the mushroom life cycle, you will be able to figure out what is wrong with your mushrooms if they are failing to produce, and you will be able to fix the problem because of your extensive knowledge on the subject. It also forces you to learn the terminology that you would most likely ignore, and knowing these terms will help you become a better hunter and ID'er.

1. Inoculation

When spores are released from the mushroom, they fall upon the right substrate or growing medium, and if the conditions are extremely favorable, the spores will germinate and start to grow. There are many circumstances in which mushrooms will not form properly, and this is why there are millions of spores that are released from the mushroom to find a suitable location to host.

2. Spore Germination

Hyphae, as we discussed earlier, will start to grow from the spores. These hyphae start to work together to create mycelium. Nutrients will start to be absorbed and collect into the center of the mushrooms colony to start creating more hyphae and eventually make a fruiting body, which we usually call a mushroom.

3. Mycelial Expansion

Mycelium is a large network of cells that works to provide nutrients for the whole mushroom. The mushroom we normally think of, a cap and stem, is actually the fruit of the organism, while the mycelium is the plant that works to supply the fruit body with nutrients. As the mycelium develops, it breaks down nearby organic matter and absorbs nutrients from its surroundings. The mycelium will then start to grow at an exponential rate as it goes up against a large number of predators nearby. It will then use many different enzymes and compounds in which to repel these predators and competitors, such as the immune system does for humans and other organisms.

4. Primordia

Mycelium then forms into hyphal knots in crowded areas in the mycelium expansion, also called primordia. This is always a welcome sign to any mushroom cultivator or grower because it means that mushrooms will soon be appearing in the near future. Primordia are also known as baby mushrooms.

5. Primordia Formation

The mushroom organism then produces more enzymes and optimizes both the mycelium and fruit body. This is the stage where much of the nutrients, antioxidants, and other good health benefits are formed, so this is a very important part of the overall process of growing mushrooms. If something were to happen to the mushroom at this stage, it would lose out on many different health benefits, so be careful at this stage in mushroom development when you are growing them.

6. Fruitbody Selection

From the millions of different primordia, the growing organism has to select the most promising primordia to allow them to grow to maturity and thus bring about the rest of the DNA to new organisms.

7. Mature Fruit Body

The new organism channels all of its energy to develop the mature fruit body. This will finally be able to produce spores that are needed to reproduce more mushrooms in the future sexually. This is the chief end of the mushroom life cycle, as in the next phase, the spores will be released.

8. Spore Release

The spores are then released into the environment, looking for a suitable substrate on which to grow and start the cycle all over again.

CHAPTER 4
GROWING MUSHROOMS

This is the amazing next step for anyone that is interested in mushrooms! I hope that my readers can get to this step and start the process of growing their own mushrooms. Here I will lay out several different mushrooms that you can grow on your own as well as the most popular ways to grow your mushrooms yourselves.

Common Mushrooms to Grow

Here I have provided a list of mushrooms that are common to grow and within reason to be easy ones to grow as well.

Maitake

<u>What It Is</u>

Its Latin name is *Grifola Frondosa;* this mushroom grows at the base of trees, those trees mostly being oaks in early autumn. This is what is known as a cluster mushroom, given how it grows in such a way. It is also a very large mushroom in comparison to others on this list. Maitake means Dancing Mushroom in its native origin of Japan, which is said to have been named after it was discovered in the woods and the people who discovered it dance with happiness because of its healing properties. It is also called the Hen of the Woods because of what it looks like.

Where it is grown/Seasons

This mushroom grows wildly in most of China and Japan, and in parts of the North American continent. It can be found in the wild around Oak and Maple trees and sometimes Elm trees in the autumn months. It grows best in the wild but can also be used at home. At home, it grows best in grow bags with the correct substrate (straw is best for this and most other mushrooms).

What it is used for

These mushrooms have equal use as a medicine and supplement as they do a portion of food for famous restaurants and tasty dishes. It has shown to lower cholesterol and be effective in fighting against cancer. So, it is effective at helping against type 2 diabetes as well as destroying cancer cells.

Taste

It goes well in soups because of its powerful umami flavor. These are some of the most sought after mushrooms for their taste and many health benefits. It also goes well as a soup stock from personal experience. Being cooked in foil with butter is also a great way to eat them. There are plenty of different ways to cook this mushroom, but this is one of the best and easiest ways to do so.

Health Benefits

Many more studies are needed to understand its effects on humans, but research is very promising with maitake mushroom. It has shown the ability to fight cancer and destroy cancer cells, lower cholesterol, and having a positive effect on type 2 diabetes as well. Also, they are overall very effective in improving the function of the immune system and regulating blood pressure.

How to Grow + Ease of Growth

These are a bit difficult to grow, but substrate in a grow bag is the most effective way to grow this mushroom. The fruit in later summer through the fall, so room temperature inside seems to be the most effective way to grow them. They are relatively difficult to grow but well worth the hassle.

Unique Facts of Each

They can get to up to 25 pounds or so on average, being a very large fungus. They have also been known to get up to 100 lbs in Japan, becoming known as the "King of Mushrooms."

They are one of the most sought after culinary-type mushrooms in the world.

These are most famously known for their cancer-fighting ability.

Maitake Mushrooms (see above)

Enoki

<u>What It Is</u>

Flammulina velutipes is a well-known part of Japanese cooking, commercially farmed as long, white mushrooms that have a distinctive crunch to them. They are also known as Golden Needle mushrooms or Futu Mushrooms. They range from being red to white, depending on the level of cultivation that has occurred.

Where it is grown/ Seasons

It is native to Japan but can easily be grown indoors in any season. It does best in the fall and can be found around the North American continent now because of European traders and travelers bringing them over with them as they migrated to the Americas.

What it is used for

It is mostly used as a culinary mushroom, being used in soups, salads, and other dishes. They, like most other mushrooms, are a wonderful source of antioxidants.

Taste

They have a delicate, crunchy taste that is very distinctive. This mushroom is a wonderful addition to any stir fry or soup. They go great with garlic and scallion sauce, as well as with shrimp. A few of the recipes listed below use this mushroom.

Health Benefits

This mushroom, like most, is full of antioxidants and has been used on animals to inhibit cancer growth and in the development of certain vaccines. This antioxidant called ergothioneine can be taken orally for extra health benefits and concentration of the antioxidant.

How to Grow + Ease of Growth

Many starter kits help you grow these small mushrooms, so try one of them out and keep them in the dark and dank area where they can flourish. Many growers use water bottles and are grown in a sawdust substrate. Follow the steps provided in a later chapter. Just be sure to keep the humidity very high for the early stages.

Unique Facts of Each

They look completely different in the wild from the cultivated adaptations of themselves. Humans have completely changed them for their own purposes.

These mushrooms tend to take longer to mature, about 90 days after you begin growing them.

Enoki (see above)

Oyster

<u>What It Is</u>

Also known as *Pleurotus ostreatus*, these are some of the most common mushrooms to be cultivated in the world. They can also be called pearl oyster mushrooms or tree oyster mushrooms.

<u>History of Mushroom</u>

First cultivated by German soldiers during WW2, there has been an outstanding increase in the number of mushrooms sold around the world. This is because they are very easy to cultivate yield a massive number of mushrooms with a small amount of work added to them. We will go through the specifics later in this book.

Where it is grown/ Seasons

These are able to be grown every season in different parts of the world, and they are known to be a very good indoor crop to grow for novice mushroom growers. They are now found naturally in the Americas for their hardiness and ability to withstand cold weather.

What it is used for

The most popular use for mushrooms is to sauté or stir-fry them, especially with butter and oil under very high heat. They are wonderful as a topping for toast, in pasta, sauces, and risotto. There are also a rising number of health benefits for oyster mushrooms in the western world of science, many of which focus on cancer and virus research.

Taste

They are a beloved favorite for their mild and savory flavor that goes with basically any dish. They go wonderfully in a sauté with garlic and green onions with a bit of oil. Once they turn golden brown, they are ready to go. There is also a very strong earthy taste to them because of their mild flavor. Frying, roasting, and grilling are all great choices with this mushroom because they tend to hold up their texture under extreme heat. Keep in mind that they are about 80% water and will shrink when they are cooked, so don't be surprised when they change shape dramatically. A few of the recipes listed below use this mushroom.

Health Benefits

One cup of raw oyster mushrooms has about 30 calories and 4 grams of protein, a stable in a vegan and vegetarian lifestyle. They have many vitamins, including phosphorus, copper, and potassium. There is a small bit of research that claims that they inhibit the growth of cancer cells, much like other mushrooms. They also help to boost the immune system and provide ample strength against viruses. For being one of the more common mushrooms, they are also dramatically one of the best mushrooms for your immune system.

How to Grow + Ease of Growth

The process by which people grow oyster mushrooms is outlined in a later chapter, and the reason this is the most common cultivated mushroom is because of the fast production methods and benefits associated with growing these mushrooms. They grow extremely fast and have a huge yield at the end of their growing period. This mushroom is good for beginners and veterans.

Unique Facts of Each

There are many oyster mushrooms in the wild, but they were first cultivated by the Germans during WW2 to be used as extra rations during the failing war effort.

There has been an increase of about 18-fold between the years 1965 and 1997 for the production of oyster mushrooms because of faster production methods and the interest in health benefits associated with these mushrooms.

Oyster Mushroom (see above)

Shiitake

<u>What It Is</u>

MUSHROOMS

The Latin name being *Lentunula Edodes,* these are one of the most famous mushrooms in the world, and for a good reason.

History of Mushroom

Shiitake has historically been used as a mouth rinse for dental plaque, as welled to treat HIV/AIDS and eczema. Also known as the Forest mushroom or the Champignon Noir. This mushroom was used by monks as a meat substitute when they fasted from meat for religious reasons.

Where it is grown/ Seasons

They are native to Asia, with different species grow at different times of the year, some in the cold and some in the warm.

What it is used for

They are used in many fancy dishes in Japan as well as common dishes such as salads and soups, and they are used as a supplement for cancer patients in China. They are a huge source of vitamin D if harvested correctly, as well.

Taste

They are extremely meaty, with a mild flavor that is close to Umami. This is a truly delicious mushroom.

This is a wonderful mushroom to have when you are fasting from meat or going vegan. A few of the recipes listed below use this mushroom.

Health Benefits

These mushrooms have been shown to lower cholesterol, help with weight loss, and boost the immune system. One of the most helpful and delicious mushrooms out there. They are also low in calories and sodium, having plenty of B vitamins as well.

How to Grow + Ease of Growth

These mushrooms are a bit more challenging to grow because their mycelium is not as easy to grow as varieties such as oyster mushrooms, but the result is well worth it if you put the time in to see them through. They grow in flushes, meaning they continue to produce after you first plant them, sometimes for years and years under the right conditions. The most important thing to remember when growing these mushrooms is that they a wood-based substrate to grow properly.

Unique Facts of Each

Shiitake mushrooms can produce every five weeks for five years if done right.

Shiitake mushrooms grow best on fresh logs.

MUSHROOMS

Submerge the logs you plan on planting in cold water for a full day.

You can drastically boost the vitamin D content in your shiitake mushrooms by putting them gill side up in a sunny location for 24 to 48 hours after you harvest them.

Shiitake Mushrooms (see above)

Lion's Mane

<u>What It Is</u>

Under the name, *Hericium Erinaceus*, this mushroom is also known as satyr's beard, bearded hedgehog, pom-pom mushroom, monkey's head mushroom, and many other names. It is edible as well as medicinal.

MUSHROOMS

History of Mushroom

Native Americans were first known to use this mushroom for medical purposes.

Where it is grown/ Seasons

It is native to North America as well as Europe and Asia, and it grows during late summer on mainly American Beech trees. It comes with no distinct cap, lacks a stipe, and is parasitic.

What it is used for

Mostly used for medical purposes, it also has been used as a substitute for seafood.

Taste

Many people call the flavor a bit like seafood, such as a lobster taste. Lions Mane is a good meat substitute.

Health Benefits

One of the most well-known health benefits to these fungi is their ability to fight against dementia and overall fight for cognitive health. Two special compounds, hericenones and erinacines, are known to stimulate the growth of brain cells. This mushroom has also been wonderful in its effectiveness against depression and anxiety in patients with chronic inflammation. Other health benefits include protection against ulcers, reduction of heart disease risks, management of diabetic symptoms, and boosting the immune system.

How to Grow + Ease of Growth

The best way to grow one of these mushrooms is to buy a kit and start that way. They are actually very easy to grow and tend to produce a few rounds of mushrooms, just make sure that you are watching their humidity.

Unique Facts of Each

This mushroom looks just like a lion's mane.

Native Americans used this as a substitute for seafood in more North-Eastern tribes.

MUSHROOMS

Lion's Mane (see above)

Wine Cap

What It Is

Also known as *Stropharia rugoso-annulata*, these mushrooms are mostly eaten when they are very young. According to leading mycologists, the white cap mushroom has no poisonous look-alikes, so this mushroom is relatively easy to forge, but always use proper precautions. They also have the name "Godzilla Mushroom."

History of Mushroom

They are historically known to be used to enrich Gardens by providing protein through their mycelium. These mushrooms are first cultivated in the late 1960s in Germany and can be found in Farmers markers in all parts of the United States as well as Europe Asia and even New Zealand.

Where it is grown/ Seasons

These mushrooms flourish around late spring and early fall but can be grown indoors all year round.

What it is used for

There are many uses for wine cap mushrooms. They are most commonly used in grilling and sautéing, and when they are young, they can be used because of their texture in stir-fries. They pair exceptionally well with nutmeg, quinoa, pasta, lemon, and wine. They can be served with meat (especially fish) and added to soups and salads.

Taste

The stems can be cooked to a crispy flavor, and have a mild and earthy, nutty flavor that tastes somewhat of red wine, giving it its name. Some people even say that it tastes somewhat like potatoes, but I digress.

Health Benefits

Wine cap mushrooms are a great provider of fiber and vitamin D, in addition to as protein copper and some calcium as well.

How to Grow + Ease of Growth

These mushrooms are most commonly grown in home gardens, oh, and they are very easy to grow if you have the right substrate. They grow best with straw and sawdust and can be used to benefit other vegetables in your gardens, such as corn or wheat.

Unique Facts of Each

They will keep for up to a week if stored in a refrigerator after harvest.

They have a very unusual flavor, and that is why it is so popular for chefs to use in their dishes.

When it is young, the cap will be a bit purple but will become brownish overtime. You should also get a purple spore print if you choose to do one of those.

Growing a Mushroom

This activity is a deeply satisfying one, and I am excited for you to start trying out the art of growing your own food or medicine. It is truly a fulfilling thing to provide for oneself, so read the next section carefully so that you can do the right things to provide the most mushrooms possible for your ability. We start by laying down a substrate, pasteurization of the soil, incubation, and then finally harvesting. This whole process should take around a few weeks.

For this example, we will discuss how to grow specifically an oyster mushroom, one of the easiest mushrooms to grow. Many of these tips apply to all mushrooms for cultivation, so feel free to use this guide for other types of mushrooms as well.

Sow: Substrate and Container

It should be obvious to you now that mushrooms feed on organic matter. They do not need the sun, such as plants, because they do not have the right cells for photosynthesis to occur. Plants have chloroplasts and can make their own food while mushrooms are heterotrophic, meaning they are not able to make their own food, but instead need their food from existing sources of plant and animal matter.

This is where the substrate comes in. The word substrate is extremely broad, but in this example, it relates to the organic material used to grow mushrooms on. Most substrates are full of nitrogen and excellent for overall plant growth. These are known as "Greens" when it comes to composting, such as peat moss, manure, hay, cocoa seeds, coffee grounds, grass clippings, etc. The best option for a beginner is anything inexpensive and local, so you can cut down on any invaders. **Straw is probably the best pick for any level.**

As for the container that you use, there are hundreds of different choices, such as a laundry basket, a potato sack, a box, a pair of shoes, a bucket, etc. Just make sure that the container has holes that allow for drainage of water as well as aeration for oxygen flow.

This is why mushrooms are so extremely sustainable; they can literally be grown in dung. Growers just need to make sure that the substrate they are using is full of nitrogen, at a good and neutral pH level, and properly fermented at a temperature of around 170 F. At this point, the compost substrate should look very brown and smell like ammonia. This leads us to pasteurization.

Steam Pasteurization

To alleviate the troubles of pests and unwanted fungi invaders, the best thing to do is to treat the substrate by exposing it to hot water or steam to pasteurize it. Without doing this, your harvests will be sporadic and inconsistent. The ammonia that was created in phase one should be used by good microbes to make a protein that is helpful for mushrooms to be food for the mushrooms. You can place your substrate in a pillowcase and allow boiling water to kill the rest of the microbes inside the substrate. The substrate can then be allowed to dry off. Eliminate as much water as possible, because leaving any extra water in the substrate will not be helpful to the growth of mushrooms.

MUSHROOMS

Next, you need to make sure your substrate is safe by decontaminating all surfaces you have touched and then lay the substrate on the table you are using to bring it all down to room temperature.

Spawn and its Issues

Mycelium will be produced from the billions of spores that are released by the mushrooms inside your substrate to create spawn. You will inoculate your substrate by adding the spawn to the substrate. Put the spawn in a clean bucket as you wait for the substrate to cool. Immediately afterward, alternate 1 to 2 inches of the substrate with .5 inches of spawn. Mix and repeat. The spawn should be on top. You can also mix the substrate and spawn so that the spawn is on top and then spread the mixture around and put it in the container you have chosen You then need to make sure that you are maintaining moisture inside of the mixture, as mycelium spreads and grows over the substrate (this is also called colonization).

Incubation

You can do this by putting your container in a trash bag, keeping the top open so that air can move around inside of the container, and then put the bag in a dark area that stays at a consistent 60-85 degrees F. After two weeks you should start to see small mushrooms called primordia forming, and then you should move your mushrooms to a new suitable location.

Conditions for a New Location

Here is a shortlist of conditions that are important in the creation of mushrooms at this stage, and if any of these conditions are not met, then you will have less than perfect mushrooms.

- Light: You need enough light so that you can read in it but not in direct sunlight

- Temperature: 60-80 degrees

- Humility: High. This will result in much bigger mushrooms, so be sure to cover your container with a clear trash bag to still allow for aeration but keep the heat and water moisture inside. Mist water 1-2 times a day inside the bag.

- Airflow: Cut about a dozen half-inch holes in the bag to create a good airflow for the mushrooms

Harvest

About 3-5 days after your primordia sprout, you should be ready to harvest. Mushrooms tend to grow exponentially, meaning that once they hit a certain growth, they expand out wildly. Oyster mushrooms grow in clusters, and once the largest mushroom has an upward curve to it, that is an indication that the mushroom is ready to be harvested. This is because the mushroom is getting ready to release its spores.

Different Ways to Grow Mushrooms

You can grow your own mushrooms from scratch!

Buy some white button or oyster mushrooms from the store. Then you need to get your hands on some coffee grounds and then boil the grounds for about 20 minutes to make sure they are sterilized. Make sure that your hands are clean as well to guard against cross-containments.

Pour a good amount of coffee grounds into the jar that you have prepared. You can put the coffee ground as well as the filter right into the mixture; the mycelium will go right through the paper. Make sure that you are applying rubbing alcohol to EVERYTHING; on your hands, the jars, the coffee filters, your hands again. EVERYTHING EVERY TIME. **You want as much sterility as possible for the mushrooms to grow effectively. This is the most important part of growing your own mushrooms.** You will put the mushrooms into the jars with coffee grounds covered by a coffee filter and a cap. Before this, however, you need to cut off the stem butt, or the bottom of the stem and then plant them into the coffee mixture. Make sure that the mycelium part is facing downwards towards the coffee grounds. The lid with the coffee filter will allow for proper airflow. After about eight days, you can then cover the mycelium with another layer of coffee grounds. Try to smother the mycelium, but allow it to be covered so that the mycelium can spread. Repeat this process until the jar is completely filled.

To clearly identify contamination, which is known as green mold, it will start off really small and then will spread out throughout the whole container if the green mold is not removed in time. This mold will attack the mycelium and destroy the colony. A good way to mitigate this damage to have about a dozen colonies of mycelium in a dozen different jars at a time to be most effective. It might be helpful to put some straw in your mixture of coffee grounds to make the situation go a bit faster.

Now, you will be able to separate the mycelium from the jar and transfer it to the straw. First, you need to cut your straw into quarter-inch lines and pour the straw into a bucket to sterilize it with hot water. You should make sure to submerge the straw completely, and then push the substrate down for a while, making sure the temperature is around 160. Always feel able to add more hot water to the substrate to keep the temperature where it needs to be. You will then remove the substrate from the water and make sure the substrate straw is nice and dry. You can use a variety of products to do this. You will then wipe down a plastic bag and fill it with the straw and then the mycelium that you have been growing. Open up the jar and pour the contents onto a plate to get the whole mycelium and coffee ground mixture out. You can tell it is ready on the coffee grounds now smell like mushrooms.

Place layer by layer of mycelium and straw at a time to make sure that the mushroom has a consistent place to go in. Poke holes in the bag to allow for aeration to occur and where the mushrooms will come out. Mist the bag every day once or twice to give it the best chance to grow.

CHAPTER 5

WAYS TO USE MUSHROOMS

This chapter by no means holds an exhaustive list of all the benefits of using mushrooms in your daily life, but it is truly a wonderful start. This information has been sourced out to many different scientific studies and professional surveys, so you can know you are getting the best information research has to offer. We will first go through a list of more than 40 ways to use and benefit from mushrooms, and then we will talk about a good number of recipes that mushrooms can be used for. Listing the benefits of mushrooms, in general, is a bit like listing the benefits of eating animals or vegetables. Because the subject matter is so broad, and there are over 200 edible species of mushrooms in the world, of course, there are so many benefits to mushrooms and using them in your personal life. This, of course, does not take away from the fact that mushrooms are extremely healthy for you as plants and animals are for you, and as processed foods are not overall good for you.

A List of Benefits

There are plenty of different ways to use mushrooms, whether it be for healing, eating, cooking for others, or disease prevention. It's no wonder why so many Eastern cultures have glorified mushrooms to such a degree. They are used in every culture from Native American to Japanese culture, from Norwegian to Icelandic cultures. This chapter will consist of a list of 42 uses for mushrooms, with information gathered from many different scholars, articles, research projects, and scientific studies. This list will be all you ever need when it comes to what you can use mushrooms for.

There is no particular order to this list, but all of these objects have been researched well and found to be true through anecdotal evidence as well. It is safe to say that all of these have been tested by multiple people, myself included, and that has allowed them to be on this list of about 43 uses and benefits for mushrooms. There are plenty more uses and reasons to grow mushrooms, but I hope that these will help you to see the reason why you should grow them in the first place. Even one of these reasons, taken in isolation, is a good enough reason for you to put these mushrooms on your shelf and get ready to use them and grow them. If you have any further questions, there should be a good amount of research done on the subject online if you are interested.

Here is a shortened list of the benefits thus listed below for your previewing. Hopefully, this will help you in finding what you are looking for quicker.

1. Fights Against Hair Loss

MUSHROOMS

2. Restores the Color of Your Hair
3. Get Rid of Dandruff
4. Lowering Cholesterol
5. Fighting Breast Cancer
6. Diabetic Diets
7. Building the Immune System
8. Helping with Weight Loss
9. Source of Vitamin B1
10. Source of Vitamin B2
11. Source of Vitamin D
12. Source of Vitamin B3
13. Source of Vitamin B5
14. Source of Vitamin B6
15. Source of Vitamin B9
16. Source of Vitamin H
17. Treatment of Skin Conditions
18. Fighting Against Aging
19. Helps Treat Acne
20. Helps Lighten Hair
21. Hydration of Skin
22. Destruction of Cancer Cells
23. Destruction of Viruses and Bacteria
24. Cleaning Polluted Soil
25. Restoration of Habitats by Polluting Factories
26. Potential Source of Fuel?
27. Used Instead of Styrofoam
28. Killing Kings
29. Promotion of Heart Health
30. Boiling

31. Frying
32. Stir Fry
33. Raw
34. Grilling
35. Sautéing
36. Help Support Liver and Kidney Function in Your Pets
37. Prevent Viral Infections in Your Pets
38. Contains Many Antioxidants
39. Garnish
40. Can produce Chitin
41. Turn Waste into Food
42. Teeth Health
43. Making Beer, Wine, and Bread

1. Fights against Hair Loss:

Mushrooms are a great source of iron, the main combatant against hair loss. This is an important mineral in the formation of red blood cells, which will, in turn, strengthen your hair cells. This fights against something called Anemia, which is the leading reason people lose their hair over time, because of a deficiency of iron in your blood. Mushrooms are great for a lot of reasons, and I bet you didn't know about this one!

2. Restores the Color of Your Hair

Because of the wonderful supply of copper in your mushrooms, this will help with the production of a pigment called melanin, which is the pigment that colors your hair. This, paired with the iron that we discussed earlier, promote strong and lively hair. Another benefit of why mushrooms are great for your hair, but that's not all.

3. Get Rid of Dandruff

Selenium is a huge part of mushrooms, and it is wonderfully effective against dandruff. This nutrient is mostly found in animals and is a very good alternative for all vegetarians to get this nutrient for their own benefit and healthy hair. As someone with a good amount of dandruff, I have found this one very helpful for dry and itchy hair.

4. Lowering Cholesterol

Many of the mushrooms that I have listed are extremely effective in lowering cholesterol in both lab tests as well as real applications on humans, so give mushrooms a try if you are struggling with your weight or heart disease.

5. Fights against Breast Cancer

Button mushrooms are extremely helpful in lowering the level of estrogen in your body so that you will be safer from breast cancer. They also suppress the level of activity of testosterone. In point 22, we will see how mushrooms help destroy cancer cells in general.

6. Diabetic Diets

Mushrooms are a wonderful source of dietary fiber, which has been known to help mitigate a number of health conditions, one of them being type 2 diabetes, given that they help lower blood glucose levels. In one cup of sliced mushrooms, there is around 1 gram of dietary fiber. 22 grams a day is recommended for adults to consume each day, so a few cups of mushrooms will give you a good boost to start your day off well.

7. Building the Immune System

Mushrooms are a wonderful choice for anyone looking to strengthen their immune system. A prime candidate for this would be the oyster mushroom, which helps drastically for this purpose. This is **probably the most useful part of mushrooms overall.** They are so packed full of nutrients that it is almost impossible to quantify how useful they are.

8. Helping with Weight Loss

Although there are few points of research to support this claim, it follows that while mushrooms are able to help regulate blood sugar and lower cholesterol levels, they should be able to contribute to weight loss in a wonderful way. Refer to points 4 and 6 on how mushrooms tend to be good for lowering cholesterol and for diabetic diets as well.

9. Source of Vitamin B1

Thiamine, also known as vitamin B1, is a wonderful additive to any diet. The shortage of Thiamine tends to create a loss of appetite, fatigue, blurry vision, vomiting, and even muscle weakness. It has been used to treat Alzheimer's disease, cataracts, and kidney disease. Thiamine can also be found in pork, poultry, bread, rice, and yeast.

10. Source of Vitamin B2

Riboflavin, also known as vitamin B2, is a vitamin found naturally in food such as eggs, green vegetables, and milk. Riboflavin is commonly taken to help prevent cancer, headaches, muscle cramps, multiple sclerosis, and even sickle cell anemia. Just like vitamin B1, it is very helpful against Alzheimer's. Riboflavin is used and required for the proper development of many different parts of the body, including the skin, brain function, and blood cells.

11. Source of Vitamin D

This vitamin is responsible for helping with the absorption of calcium, magnesium, and phosphate. It also helps maintain strong bones. It follows that if you have low levels of vitamin D, then you will have weaker bones and muscle weakness, as well. And while vitamin D is found in very few foods, mushrooms happen to have a good amount, 1 IU in 18 grams of mushrooms, more than most foods.

12. Source of Vitamin B3

Niacin, also known as vitamin B3, is used to treat high cholesterol, so it is very helpful to reduce the risk of a heart attack and the narrowing of the heart arteries. Really, Niacin is good for the overall health of the body. It is good to have 16 milligrams of niacin a day, and most mushrooms have some of the best "vegetable" sources of niacin, giving 2.5 mg per cup (70 grams). Truly, mushrooms are wonderful for overall health.

13. Source of Vitamin B5

Pantothenic acid, also known as vitamin B5, is necessary for humans to take to metabolize the major macros; carbohydrates, fats, and proteins. While research has not definitely proven any of these, vitamin B5 has been used to treat a wide range of different problems, such as acne, autism, colitis, depression, nerve pain, gray hair, obesity, headaches, and even low blood sugar. This vitamin is essential for good overall health, and mushrooms are high in B5.

14. Source of Vitamin B6

Also known as Pyridoxine, this vitamin is used for many different reasons. This vitamin has been known to help treat mood and depression, improving levels of serotonin, dopamine, and other neurotransmitters. Like many other vitamins in mushrooms, vitamin B6 is known to help with reducing the risk of Alzheimer's disease and overall promoting brain health. It has also been known to reduce the symptoms of PMS, nausea during pregnancy, reduction of heart disease risk, help prevent cancer, and finally promoting overall eye health and preventing eye diseases. This is a super vitamin if there ever was one.

15. Source of Vitamin B9

Folate, also known as vitamin B9, is mainly taken by women who are planning to become pregnant or are pregnant presently. They help the body use fats and proteins, but not necessarily carbohydrates. There are no known risks in taking vitamin B9. If you have a lack of B9 in your system, you could start to experience forgetfulness, diarrhea, loss of appetite, or shortness of breath. Mushrooms are high in this vitamin and are used by pregnant women to support the growth of the fetus.

16. Source of Vitamin H

Biotin, also known as vitamin H, is very helpful in terms of metabolic processes, mostly in the utilization of fats, carbs, and proteins. So, vitamin H is used to break down these substances in the body for them to be used for energy. Mostly found in yeast, milk, and egg yolks, this is also found in small amounts in mushrooms.

When combined with the many other health benefits of mushrooms, this is just a drop in the bucket.

17. Treatment of Skin Conditions

Skin conditions of all kinds are subject to be changed when you decide to consume mushrooms. Conditions such as eczema, acne, and even rosacea (which is the condition that results in small, pus-filled pimples on your wonderful face) can be treated by getting the right amounts of nutrients from mushrooms and extracts taken from mushrooms themselves.

18. Fighting against Aging

Kojic acid, which is also used to lighten the skin of people that eat mushrooms, is also useful as an antiaging unit in creams and lotions. Mushrooms are masters at changing the landscape of the face into what it was supposed to originally look like without any uneven skin tones, discoloration, or age spots. This is an unusual acid not found in many other places, so this is a wonderful reason to use and grow mushrooms.

19. Helps Treat Acne

Being high in Vitamin D, and we talked about why it is also so helpful later, mushrooms can help people with acne lesions. This is so helpful to the skin that some products use extracts from certain mushrooms to help treat skin conditions such as acne.

This is a wonderful, natural solution to a natural problem for many people, as well as being a great alternative to other unnatural strategies.

20. Helps Lighten Skin

Not only do mushrooms help against acne and hydrating the skin, as we will talk about later, mushrooms also have a thing called kojic acid, which is known to be a natural skin lightening agent. This acid helps to prevent the production of melanin on the surface of your skin so that your skin has the ability to lighten up instead of darkening. This is helpful for those that have that goal in mind.

21. Hydration of Skin

Mushrooms are pumped full of this thing called hyaluronic acid, which acts as the body's moisturizer for your skin. Studies have shown that it reduces fine lines and wrinkles in the skin, as well as helping against the overall aging of the skin. This will cause the skin to look nice and smooth over time.

22. Destruction of Cancer Cells

The number of antioxidants in most edible mushrooms is a wonderful surprise to many new growers. Mushrooms have been proven to help with multiple types of cancers, including prostate, breast, lung, and many other types as well. Sources have been known to suggest that the vitamin, selenium, can prevent cancer, but there are no comprehensive studies to confirm this. Vitamin D and choline are also present in most known mushrooms, and these have been known to mitigate most forms of cancer, specifical choline.

23. Destruction of Viruses and Bacteria

This has been true with the flu virus as well as many other viruses throughout research terms. Paul Stamets and his team of researchers have done extensive work on this subject for further details. This was talked about in the introduction as well for more information.

24. Cleaning Polluted Soil

In a fascinating turn of events, mushrooms are grown in a pile of diesel sludge and trash bloom (if you could call what they do blooming). But their magic doesn't stop there. They start to allow for other grasses and small plants to start growing there, as well. Insects are attracted to the plants and mushrooms, the spores from the mushrooms continue to attract bugs, and then birds start to come. They drop seeds, and this continues the cycle until what was once a pile of crap is turned into a beautiful oasis of greenery and life. One last thing: the mushrooms can be eaten, and they are completely healthy, because of all the antioxidants in them. A truly amazing turn of events for the environment. Refer to point 41 for more information.

25. Restoration of Habitats by Polluting Factories

As we have seen with the research of Paul Stamets, regular mushrooms can transform wastelands into beautiful ecosystems. This information should also be found in the introduction.

26. Potential Source of Fuel?

This has not been proven to be completely effective yet, but there is research that suggests this would be an option in the near future.

27. Used Instead of Styrofoam

In several cases, mushrooms have been known to be able to be transformed into a different source of packing material that can replace Styrofoam. While this is still a new idea and is still a difficult thing to do at this point in its development, as time goes on it should become a better and better supplemental material for Styrofoam, and hopefully one day we will be able to replace Styrofoam completely and use mushroom fibers instead. The fibers are the part of the fungus found in the stem and could prove to be even more effective than conventional packing materials in the near future.

28. Killing Kings

Refer to the introduction for an explanation of this point. Not too good for Austria, but helpful to other European countries.

29. Promotion of Heart Health

Mushrooms are full of Vitamin C and Potassium, both of which are extremely healthy and helpful in overall heart health. And while it is helpful for people with type 2 diabetes such as in point 6, it is also helpful for those that do not have that problem. Studies have concluded that people with low vitamin C would have more cardiovascular problems and even cardiovascular disease. While vitamin C supplements have not been proven to help with these problems, dietary fiber is one of the helpful fibers in mushrooms, a fiber called beta-glucans has also been proven to lower cholesterol levels. Stems of mushrooms are full of these, so be sure to add these to your diet as an extra precaution

30. Boiling

This type of cooking the fungus will allow for most of the water in the mushroom to stay where it is, as well as kill any bacteria that were resting on the mushroom.

31. Frying

A few of the recipes found in the latter part of this chapter, and it is a favorite of most Americans.

32. Stir Fry

Since most mushrooms contain about 80% water, once they are put into a wok and fried up with rice, sauce, meat, and veggies, they make a wonderful addition to any diet. They are very easy to cook and have little to no preparation time. They are also a wonderful substitute for meat, as monks and other spirituals have used for hundreds of years for meat fasts.

33. Raw

This is probably the least safe way to eat mushrooms, but if you know what types of mushrooms are good to be eaten raw, then you should be completely fine.

34. Grilling

Although this will get rid of most of the minerals and water found in mushrooms, this will be an excellent choice, especially for mushrooms such as Portabellos.

35. Sauteing

A favorite for the finer culinary tastes among us, great for several of the recipes listed below.

36. Help Support Liver and Kidney Function in Your Pets

MUSHROOMS

This was an interesting one me to see. I had no idea how mushrooms could be used for pets until I checked out this https://www.drbasko.com/portfolio-items/many-health-benefits-mushrooms-add-pets-diet.

37. Prevent Viral Infections in Your Pets

This point is also connected to the one above.

38. Contains Many Antioxidants

This is one of the best parts of the mushroom. There are so many of these in the average mushroom that one could get most of your daily needs of antioxidants in just a few cups of mushrooms a day. There are plenty of antioxidants found in mushrooms for the average person to utilize, and maybe someday, as more research comes out, be used as a medicine alongside modern medicine and research.

39. Garnish

Mushrooms are best served cut up into smaller pieces, and finding themselves in a salad for an added meaty kick is wonderful for any person who is going on a diet or is switching over to a vegetative diet more specifically.

40. Can produce Chitin

MUSHROOMS

Mostly helpful as dietary fiber, mushrooms have certain elements that can be used to make Chitin, which is also a food thickening agent.

41. Turn Waste into Food

In a fascinating turn of events, mushrooms are grown in a pile of diesel sludge and trash bloom (if you could call what they do blooming). But their magic doesn't stop there. They start to allow for other grasses and small plants to start growing there, as well. Insects are attracted to the plants and mushrooms. The spores from the mushrooms continue to attract bugs, and then birds start to come. They drop seeds, and this continues the cycle until what was once a pile of crap is turned into a beautiful oasis of greenery and life. One last thing: the mushrooms can be eaten, and they are completely healthy, because of all the antioxidants in them.

42. Teeth Health

Multiple studies have shown that mushrooms can help clean teeth because of the minerals found in them, and extracts from mushrooms have also been found in certain types of toothpaste.

43. Making Beer, Wine, and Bread

Saccharomyces, also known as yeast, is completely necessary when it comes to making beer, wine, and bread. This is perhaps the most important reason fungi are used for over thousands of years of human development, albeit not the overall healthiest, but not specifically unhealthy at all. Without yeast, who knows what humankind would look like.

MUSHROOMS

CHAPTER 6

FORAGING AND IDENTIFICATION

Overall, when it comes to identification, mushroom growers need to be careful in their selection of mushrooms and be ready to take extra precautions to be as safe as possible.

This book is primarily about mushroom growing and using, but this is also an important part of being a holistic mushroom lover.

There are a couple of old sayings when it comes to foraging for mushrooms:

"There are old mushroom foragers and bold mushroom foragers, However, there are no old, bold mushroom foragers."

"All hunters put life at risk, but for mushroomers, the moment of danger comes well after the quarry has been run to the ground...Finding the mushroom is the initiation, but eating it is the test." - John Thorne

Foraging for mushrooms has been a habitat of human beings in virtually every country for thousands of years at one point or another. Some cultures do so to find fungi to add to their otherwise weak diets, such as parts of Africa. Others, such as in Nepal, forage for mushrooms because of the money to be made, some foragers being able to make nearly half a year's salary during one growing season. Besides the economic reasons, there is also the fun of the act itself! In England, when schooling had become mandatory, teachers would let students go home early to explore the woods with their mothers to search for mushrooms for food as well as for a learning exercise.

As we have understood throughout this book, there are many ways to use mushrooms for health benefits and other reasons as well that we still don't have enough space to talk about. It serves one best to explore the benefits of them oneself. Mushrooms are wonderfully fun to search for on a cool autumn morning, and the thrill of the search is only added to the benefits given to the forager upon consuming the mushroom itself. This is considered better than cultivating your own mushrooms to some because of the thrill of the "quiet hunt" (as coined by Antonio Carluccio in his book *The Complete Mushroom Book* in 2003)

MUSHROOMS

Jean-Jacques Paulet made the first useful guide in the 1790s to assist the flourish of new foragers looking for adventure in the woodlands of France. Since then, we have advanced in many ways in the expansion of learning how to identify mushrooms better. I would suggest getting a good guidebook that is sufficient for the area you hope to be foraging in. This will take a lot of grief off of you and make you feel safer in your foraging, which should be more of an enjoyable activity.

Here is a list of questions you should ask when you find a mushroom in the field and are not sure about its origin or its name:

- Where is it growing?
- How is it growing?
- Is it growing in a cluster?
- Is it growing by itself?
- What color is its cap, gills, base, etc.?
- Is the base straight, or is it bulbous?
- Does it have a sac?
- What does the mushroom feel like?
- What does it smell like?

MUSHROOMS

There are not many tools that a forager needs in their collection. The most important tool you can have is a magnifying glass and a knife, the magnifying glass for helping to identify certain characteristics of the mushroom, and the nice for cutting stems. Other tools that are necessary for foraging are some sort of tool to dig with a basket for keeping all the different species separate, rubber boots, etc. Some forgers find that using something called a Spore bag works very well to prevent any damaging to the artist that they have; this will also get rid of any creatures that want to come home with you in the mushroom caps. As there are also rules for identification, you should always check out the size, the color, the gill connectivity, the cross-section, bruising color, odor spore print, and environments of the mushroom before being absolutely certain of its original name.

A few things to keep in mind when looking for those tasty edibles in your next quiet hunt for mushrooms. *Only eat mushrooms that you are completely sure about.* You need to learn about both edible mushrooms as well as poisonous mushrooms to tell them apart from each other. Take the time to study your guide for a good amount of both edible and poisonous mushrooms to be as safe as possible on your next adventure. Next, *don't be hasty in your selection and take your time.* You need to pick the **entire** mushroom to make a positive identification. The base of the mushroom needs to be shown for a good identification to be made. The second thing to do with this mushroom, if you are not absolutely sure about the nature of the mushroom, is to take a spore print, especially with grilled mushrooms. Next, *eat only a small bit of the mushroom at first to make sure you are not adversely affected by the mushroom.* Even if the mushroom is not poisonous to most people, it may be disagreeable with you and your body. It is better to be safe rather than sorry.

CHAPTER 7

THE POWER OF A MEDICINAL MUSHROOM

Mushrooms are one of the most nutrient-dense foods in the world, providing the bacteria in our gut with unique types of fiber not found in any other foods. Recently, a new trend has kicked off, discussions about medicinal mushrooms, the power they have and what they can do for us.

A medicinal mushroom is a subcategory that, as well as having a great taste and plenty of nutrients, is also packed with proven medicinal benefits. The big question is, do they live up to the hype? In short, yes, they do, and that is what we're going to be talking about in this chapter.

Medicinal mushrooms have long been used in traditional medicine for centuries and across many different cultures. In contrast to many of the other alternative medicine products and techniques, medicinal mushrooms are the subject of hundreds of studies and have long been validated as having beneficial effects. Somewhere along the line, I'm sure you heard that your immune system could benefit from medicinal mushrooms, but was you also aware that they provide great benefits for the cardiovascular system, your blood sugar, endocrine system, and so much more? They can even help you to fight fatigue!

Before we dive into all that, though, we need to take a quick look at the basics.

What is a Medicinal Mushroom?

You already know that a mushroom is the fruit body of different species of fungus. Fungi have their own kingdom and are an important organism that plays a vital role in every ecosystem. Specifically, they contribute to the decay of animal and plant matter, as well as recycling it. Mushrooms have long been studied for the compounds that make up their unique ability to digest and recycle other organisms.

So, why are medicinal mushrooms so-called? Because there have been many studies on their abilities to sustain and improve life. At current, there are about 700 species deemed to have the right properties to be called medicinal. That said, not every one of those species is backed up by scientific studies, at least not yet.

However, there are some very well-known species long used in traditional cultures, particularly Asian cultures, but also in parts of Africa and Eastern Europe; these mushrooms do have the scientific backing and include:

- Chaga (*Inonotus obliquus*)
- Cordyceps (*Cordyceps Sinensis*)
- Lion's Mane (*Hericium Erinaceus*)
- Reishi (*Ganoderma lucidum*)
- Shiitake (*Lentinus edodes*)
- Turkey Tail (*Trametes Versicolor*)

This is just a tiny example of the more than 14,000 mushroom species and up to 10 million fungi species around the world, so what has been studied is the tip of the iceberg, so to speak.

Physiological Effects of a Medicinal Mushroom

Medicinal mushrooms come with many benefits, lots of them physiological, and we're going to look at the ways they can benefit our health. All of these are backed up by years of scientific studies.

The Immune System

The immune system is the most well-known mechanism backing up the effects of these mushrooms, and most of us will have read some news stories about the immunomodulating and anti-tumor effects of medicinal mushrooms. But there's more to it than that.

MUSHROOMS

There are other physiological actions identified over the years, demonstrating just how potent these mushrooms are on the immune system.

Antitumor – more than 30 types of medicinal mushrooms contain polysaccharides that have been proven to help prevent tumors from forming. They also exhibit direct activity against tumors and can also stop metastasis, which is when cancer spreads from the originating organ to one or more other organs or locations in the body. More specifically, scientific research shows that those effects are even stronger when they are used together with chemotherapy, and both can be used safely at the same time. T cells modulate the activity, so the person's thymus and T cell system need to be intact.

Immunomodulating – Some medicinal mushrooms contain components that can induce a genetic expression. This then leads to several immunomodulatory cytokine receptors and cytokines being created, allowing the immune system to provide the right response to stressors and damping down unwanted inflammation.

Antioxidants and Free Radical Scavengers - these scavengers are compounds that can neutralize both oxidized compounds and free radicals in the human body. Antioxidants also go to work in the liver enzymes vita for elimination and detoxification. Some medicinal mushroom compounds have also been discovered to have an incredibly potent capacity in terms of antioxidants, and this most certainly plays a part in both anti-inflammatory and antitumor properties.

Antifungal, Antiparasitic, and Antibacterial – there are now studies that make comparisons between the antimicrobial activities in medicinal mushrooms with those of antibiotics produced by the pharmaceutical industry. Right now, it is thought that to stay vital out in nature, mushrooms need antimicrobial properties, and, when we consume the mushrooms, we also get some of those benefits. What is interesting is that some studies now show shiitake mushrooms to be antimicrobial agents fighting infections that are often resistant to treatment, such as E.coli 0157:H7, and shigella.

Anti-Inflammatory – while some of the categories discussed above already count as being anti-inflammatory but it's worth highlighting that medicinal mushrooms, in general, are considered to have excellent anti-inflammatory properties. Some of the polysaccharides have been shown to exhibit anti-inflammatory activity, including phenols, terpenoids, and proteoglycans.

It's worth diverting our attention for a moment to look at what this could mean for the way autoimmune diseases are managed and looking at a few of the concepts in detail. Mushrooms contain a fibrous component called beta-glucans, and these have the potential to be bioactive. The beta-glucans are tiny molecules and can easily bind directly to immune cells.

Because of that, they affect immune activity, together with the indirect effects of the gut microbiome.

It was this that was responsible for the rationale behind the avoidance of using medicinal mushrooms or their extracts on the AIP – the autoimmune protocol. Anyone who suffers from an autoimmune disease must be very wary of anything that may have a stimulating effect on their immune system but, in recent times, more studies have been done. These now show that medicinal mushrooms are not immunostimulatory; instead, they are immunomodulatory, which means they rebalance an immune system that is out of kilter. One of the best-studied mushrooms in this area is the reishi mushroom.

Studies done on patients with rheumatoid arthritis showed a decrease in joint pain alongside a reduction in interleukin(IL)-18 – this has a potent activation effect on TH1 cells, and the same studies showed that cytokines, like measured inflammatory cells, did not increase. Another study of lupus in mice showed that a supplement containing reishi extract brought about a decrease in autoantibodies and an increase in survival rates.

Yet another lupus mouse study demonstrated that reishi increased the regulatory T cell ratio to both TH1 and TH17 cells, alongside cytokine changes, such as Il-10, IL-17, and IL-21 decreases and IL2, and IL-12P70 increases.

Lastly, a mouse model based on Alzheimer's disease demonstrated gene expression changes correlating to a decrease in the activity of the disease, thanks to supplementation with reishi. What is truly fascinating is that the reishi extract has also been shown to help in cancer, increasing the T cell (cytotoxic) activity, as well as having an effect on angiogenesis and the growth of cancer cells.

All of this paints a picture of extracts of medicinal mushrooms, in particular, reishi, having huge benefits where the immune system is under-active, for example, when you have the flu or a common cold; they are also beneficial in cases of overactive function, such as the many autoimmune diseases and in fighting cancer and stopping it from metastasizing.

The Autoimmune Protocol does include whole mushrooms, such as the shiitake, but there is a clear need for more confirmatory research before extracts may be given a definitive go-ahead for those with autoimmune diseases. For now, it's probably best to avoid them

The Cardiovascular System

Medicinal mushrooms have also been shown to be beneficial to the cardiovascular system. As it is with the immune system, studies have been done, showing they help in combatting some diseases while providing preventative benefits at the same time. Some species are proven to assist in the treatment of ischemic heart disease, the commonest cause of a heart attack, of chronic heart failure, and arrhythmia. It is the anti-inflammatory benefits of medicinal mushrooms that increase the dilation in the blood vessels and increases the blood circulation to the heart. And it works the same way for circulation to the brain too.

It has also been shown that medicinal mushroom supplementation can lower LDL cholesterol, total cholesterol, and inhibit the time taken for platelet aggregation, which prevents plaque. All of this works towards preventing heart disease, and one of the best-known mushrooms for this is the cordyceps.

The Respiratory System

Clinical trials have been done on some medicinal mushrooms and their properties in improving lung health, as well as traditional usage for some lung conditions. The cordyceps mushroom, for example, has long been used as a form of treatment for asthma, bronchitis, and other respiratory disorders. Many studies have been done on patients who have asthma, and the effectiveness of the mushroom was proven after the usage for a period of five to six weeks. Another study looked at how cordyceps affected patients who had stages I, II, and III non-small cell lung cancer, and showed it was beneficial.

The Endocrine System

Blood sugar regulation is one of the most studied benefits on health that medicinal mushrooms have. The mushrooms contain fantastic prebiotics, required for the gut microbiome, and providing support for a healthy gut. Gut health is an important factor in blood sugar regulation – it isn't all about carbohydrate and sugar consumption, however, to get the best benefits, you need to consume whole mushrooms and/or whole mushrooms in powdered form. With that, you get the full impact of the unique fibers in mushrooms, called chitin, and the nutrients.

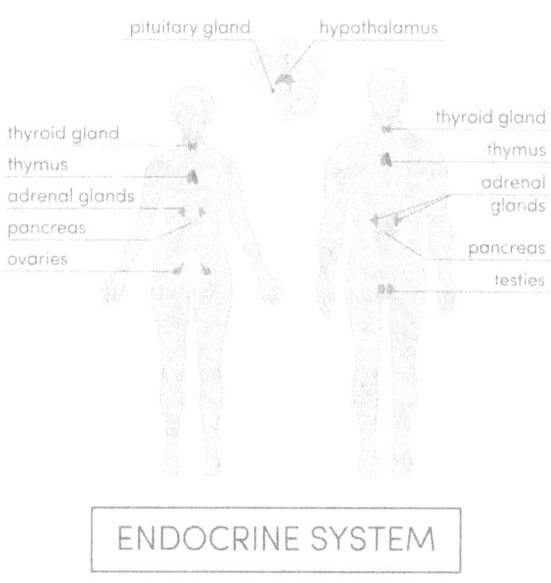

ENDOCRINE SYSTEM

Elimination and Detoxification

That covers your liver, kidneys, and your gut health. China has long used the mushroom for its benefits in treating kidney failure, chronic nephritis, and other kidney diseases. Medicinal mushrooms have been studied for their links to water balance, and this, of course, can help with kidney disease. By the same token, because they are such strong antioxidants, the medicinal mushroom is fantastic or the liver too. In short, their strong antioxidant support means that the liver doesn't have to do so much work in generating them to detoxify the cells and eliminate toxic substances.

As mentioned earlier, mushrooms contain chitin, which is a unique fiber. More importantly, it is a fermentable oligosaccharide fiber. It is comprised of long chains containing N-acetylglucosamine, which is a glucose derivative that has amino acids attached to it. We can only get this from fungi, such as medicinal mushrooms, shellfish scales, fish scales, and insect exoskeletons. As it happens, chitin is a powerful prebiotic and studies show that it helps different gut-friendly bacteria, such as Lactobacillus, Bifidobacterium, Bacteroides, and Akkermansia. At the same time, it reduces the level of Desulfovibrio, which is an inflammatory microbe commonly found in those who suffer from inflammatory bowel disease. Mice studies show that the oligosaccharides, produced when chitin is digested, modulate microbiota in the gut to fight against metabolic syndrome, induced by diet, and slowing down the rate at which the gut barrier is destroyed.

Chitosan, another fiber made up of the same molecules, also contains D-glucosamine molecules, distributed randomly throughout the chain. This is only found naturally in the cell walls o mushrooms and other fungi. Mice studies showed that it increased the diversity of gut microbes, increased levels of Bacteroides, and decreased levels of firmicute and Shigella and Escherichia, both pathogenic genera. Where the mice were diabetic, chitosan reshaped the microbiota in a bid to produce an effect that was anti-diabetic.

So, it would seem that, to keep your gut in tip-top shape, you should be eating medicinal mushrooms, whole and as natural as they grow.

General Wellbeing and Fatigue

While this isn't all that easy to measure fully in research and studies, it is an important one to include. The primary reason for that is that it is one of the most traditional and well-known uses of the medicinal mushroom. Studies show that those who regularly consume the mushrooms say they don't suffer from fatigue or exhaustion as much. The same studies on animals showed that the mushrooms promote an increase in oxygen availability to tissues and increase ATP production, the molecule used for energy in the cells.

By the same token, studies on medicinal mushrooms for supporting chemotherapy show that the side effects of the treatment are reduced when medicinal mushrooms are used alongside it.

Whole Medicinal Mushrooms or Extracts?

Right now, you can buy any number of products that contain medicinal mushrooms, and it is clear that the hype is correct. The thing is, although you can buy any product that contains the mushrooms, there are some products that are better than others – those that have the correct mushroom sourcing and extraction methods. Most of the scientific research focuses on two main extraction methods – hot water and hot water with alcohol. These methods both mimic the modern and traditional Chinese methods of preparing medicinal mushrooms.

Traditionally, decoctions have been used to prepare medicinal mushrooms; a decoction is much like a "super tea"; the mushrooms are placed in boiling water and simmered for between 20 minutes and two hours. Doing this helps to break the cellular walls of tough mushrooms, allowing the components into the water. One of those components is chitin, the main component of the fungi's cell walls. Using hot water to extract the components, with alcohol or without, is the only proper way of breaking the cell walls down and extracting the chitin that is so beneficial to the gut microbiome. And some mushrooms provide more chitin in this way than you get eating the whole mushroom.

Some products contain whole ground mushrooms. While eating whole mushrooms is recommended, the ground format isn't the subject of many studies. Where you can purchase medicinal mushrooms whole, such as the shiitake mushroom, you should add them to your food when you cook; for others, use the hot water methods for maximum benefits.

One more thing you should look out for are those extracts that are made from the whole mushroom and not just the mycelium. This is normally grown in a grain medium, and products with mycelium may well be misleading – most of the fiber is from the grain the mycelium is grown in and not from the mushrooms, which means it isn't all that beneficial. Look on the label for the beta-glucan measurement and, if there, the triterpenoid content, as well as looking for those products that have gluten-free certification.

Overall, the medicinal mushrooms do live up to their hype, and we should all be adding them, in some form or another, to our daily diets.

Six Medicinal Mushrooms to Boost your Health

For thousands of years, medicinal mushrooms have been a big part of Eastern medicine and, these days, they are growing in popularity for mainstream use. Typically, they are taken in powder form, as very few can be eaten raw or whole, medicinal mushrooms can be found in all forms. One of the best ways to get your fix is to add a spoonful of powder to whatever you are eating or drinking.

The health benefits provided by medicinal mushrooms are endless, but every mushroom is different, and each one has its own unique advantages in terms of health benefits. Do keep in mind that they are not a cure-all though and are still relatively new in Western medicine. While much research has already been done, more is needed so, for now, think of them as an addition, a helping hand in combatting stress, for boosting your immune system and fighting cancer or inflammatory diseases.

Some are better than others for certain conditions, so let's look at six medicinal mushrooms and what they can do for you.

Reishi Mushrooms Soften the Edge

Reishi is the fungi version of Xanax and is one of the more popular of the medicinal mushrooms. And there is an excellent reason for that – reishi can do so much. It helps with weight loss, ensures your immune system is working as it should be, and can even put up a fierce fight against cancer cells.

However, it's most unique property is that it is a claiming mushroom. That is down to triterpene, a compound this mushroom has in spades. Triterpene is a mood-booster, and it can help to ease depression, alleviate anxiety, help you sleep better, and more. But it doesn't stop there, Reishi also helps promote healing, and it can sharpen up your focus too.

Try using a spoonful to make a cup of healing, hot tea, or even stir it into a chocolate pudding.

Boost Your Brain with Lion's Mane

If your brain is foggy, a spot of lion's mane can clear things up for you. A 'pom-pom' mushroom is a feathery fungus full of antioxidants that can help strengthen your immune system in the way most medicinal mushrooms can. This is a rare mushroom, though, because it promotes the growth of NGF (nerve growth factor) called bioprotein, along with myelin, which is what insulates nerve fibers.

Both myelin and NFG are critical to the health of our brains; if they are not balanced, we are more at risk of neurological diseases, such as multiple sclerosis or Alzheimer's disease. Studies have also shown the lion's main mushroom helps improve cognition, alleviate irritability, anxiety, and increase concentration levels.

Add a spoon of lion's mane to yerba tea to provide a drink packed with antioxidants that clear your mind.

Use Chaga to Boost Your Antioxidants

Chaga mushrooms are one of the medicinal mushroom powerhouses, packed with antioxidants that help fight inflammation and free radicals. It is a dark black in color and helps fight against oxidative stress, which causes aging of the skin. It can also help to slow down or even prevent cancer growth, and studies have shown it lowers LDL cholesterol. Most of the research on the change mushroom has been done on mice, and human cells, and all the signs point to it being a fantastic mushroom for your health, inside your body and out.

Add a spoon of powder to a smoothie or add it to a chai latte.

MUSHROOMS

Chaga Mushroom (see above)

MUSHROOMS

Keep Your Heart Healthy With Shiitake

If you are already using shiitake mushrooms in your cooking, then good for you, but the benefits of this popular mushroom go far beyond taste.

Shiitake mushrooms are excellent for the heart and have been proven to lower LDL cholesterol. Some of their compounds inhibit the absorption of cholesterol in the liver and well as inhibiting its growth. They are also a rich source of phytonutrients, useful for stopping plaque from building up and, following studies on rats also shown to keep blood circulation and blood pressure healthy

Add a spoonful of powder to any recipe to give it a healthy, hearty boost of goodness.

Use Turkey Tail to Fight Cancer

Practically all medicinal mushrooms contain cancer-fighting properties, thanks primarily to the high level of antioxidants they contain. However, the turkey tail mushroom takes things further.

It has a compound called PSK, or polysaccharide-K. This compound is excellent at providing the immune system with stimulation and is so effective that, in Japan, it is now an approved prescription drug to fight cancer. Studies on the turkey tail mushroom show that it improves survival rates for certain cancers, can fight against leukemia and helps boost the immune systems of those undergoing chemotherapy. It is important, however, that you do NOT stop taking prescribed drugs without speaking to your doctor first.

Try adding a spoonful to a smoothie to give it an immune-boosting punch or even have a go at making a batch of turkey tail ale!

Cordyceps Is The Perfect Pick-Me-Up

If you feel like your energy is flagging or you need a boost before you work out, reach for the cordyceps. This is one of the best-known mushrooms to provide stimulation, and not just for energy levels, either – it also works on the libido!

Cordyceps is excellent at supporting efficient oxygen utilization in the body and ensuring efficient blood flow. This is one of the most helpful mushrooms or people who work out a lot, and for athletes and studies show it doesn't just improve performance, it also helps to speed up muscle recovery after working out.

Add a spoonful to your pre-workout meal for an energy boost and your post-workout meal to help hasten recovery.

The Takeaway

One of the best ways of getting the fantastic benefits from these mushrooms is to add a spoonful to your meals or drinks every day. Don't take any more than one or two tablespoons per day, though – even if you do feel much better afterward, taking more won't make a difference, and as most of these mushrooms are still under trial for their benefits its best to wait and see before you take more.

Do make sure you consult your doctor before taking any of these; you need to be sure that it is safe for you to add them, particularly if you are pregnant, nursing, or taking any other medications. Make sure you do your homework too – like anything, some mushrooms can cause allergies, stomach upsets, and other side effects.

CHAPTER 8

COMMON MISTAKES TO AVOID WHEN GROWING MUSHROOMS

Provided you follow the right steps, cultivating mushrooms is a relatively straightforward process, and you can reap the rewards for many years to come. However, it's a fact of life that things go wrong, and failures happen. It could be down to sheer bad luck, contamination, even environmental issues but, whatever causes your crop to fail, you need to step back and work out what's gone wrong.

When you troubleshoot a poor or failed crop, first look at the technique you used. It may be that you did something wrong, or it wasn't the right techniques for the particular mushroom you are trying to grow. After that, you can look at everything else. Be thorough and eliminate obvious and/or potential problems. Be careful, though; sometimes, when you fix what you think is a problem, you can make another problem worse.

Sometimes, even discovering a problem can't fix it – it might be too late to save things. Learn from it and get the next crop right. You can follow these tips to help you be more prepared:

The Problem – The Medium is Inoculated, but No Fruit is Produced

If the medium is inoculated correctly but doesn't produce any mushrooms, the first solution is simple – time. It can take more than a year for some mushroom strains to produce, and that means you need a lot of patience – something many beginners are short of. The answer is to stagger your mushroom cultivation over two or three years, and you should have a regular harvest.

That said, there are things you can do to get things moving a bit faster or give the mycelium a boost if it appears to be too slow in fruiting. The first thing is moisture. Make sure the growing medium you use, be it wood chips, logs, whatever, is misted a minimum of once per week, more in warmer, dryer times. You can also soak logs for 24 hours in cold water.

The next thing is to ensure there is sufficient airflow. Place logs outside in areas that have plenty of ventilation, with air coming from all directions, or as many as possible, anyway.

If you are cultivating mushrooms indoors, keep the windows open, or a fan switched on to keep the air flowing through the room. Although you don't need to, it might be helpful to moisten the medium and the spawn before inoculation and, immediately after inoculation, moisten the medium again, to stop the spawn drying and to hasten things.

Contaminated spawn is a problem, too, but you can avoid this by making sure you handle it carefully. Thoroughly wash your hands before you handle it, and when you take a break from inoculating the medium. Never allow the spawn to come into contact with any surface other than the medium you are using and, if you are ill, definitely do not handle the spawn. The human body plays host to many different types of bacteria, as does the environment, and all of these have the potential for contaminating the spawn, taking hold before the mycelium can become dominant.

If you can, pasteurize the medium before you inoculate it. Typically, this is only done when you use a straw. It should be heated just enough to get rid of the harmful bacteria but retain the beneficial bacteria. If you use a sterilization process, with very high heat levels, pressure, or chemicals, you will kill all the bacteria, including the good stuff, and that leaves the medium wide-open for the bad stuff to creep in again. The ideal temperature for pasteurization is 160°F to 180°F. To do it, heat water to between 160°F and 170°F and then leave the straw to soak for an hour – do maintain the temperature throughout.

Problem – The Mycelium is Growing, but there is No Fruit

If you find, when you look at your growing medium, that there are fibrous, white materials, the mycelium is growing. However, depending on the type of mushroom you are cultivating, you may have to wait a while for the fruit to appear. If you don't see any for some time after or they do start growing but then abort, there could be any number of reasons. First, you may have used the wrong match of medium and strain, or you could be using a bad strain. In the latter case, next time, choose a different strain and, in the former, do some meticulous research on what medium goes with the strain you are trying to grow. What you mustn't do, if you see tiny pins or mushrooms, is assume they have aborted - often, these will appear long before full growth is achieved.

Problem – The Substrate Doesn't Produce

Make sure you thoroughly understand the correct region for each strain, along with the growth cycle, before you decide that there is a problem. There are three primary designations for growth conditions – warm, cold, or wide-range weather. Each indicates when the strain will fruit, not the type of growing conditions. In other words, if your region is moderately temperate, all three strains could be planted, so you get a staggered harvest.

The wide-range strains tend to fruit in early spring, midsummer or late all, depending on whether your climate is southerly or northerly. The cold strains produce late fall and early spring in a northerly region and, in the southerly regions, throughout most of the winter months. And the warm strains tend to produce midsummer right through to early all in most regions.

Problem – The Mushrooms are Deformed

If you get overlong stems, caps that are cracked or underdeveloped, and other types of deformity, it may be that you don't have enough light, insufficient airflow, or too much moisture. Most mushroom strains require a level of diffused light for proper growth because, like most plants, mushrooms move towards the light when they grow.

If there isn't enough light, the stem will grow tall and spindly as it tries to push the cap towards the light; the result will also be a thin, narrow, and small cap. Too much or too little moisture may also result in problems. Never allow logs to stand in water or leave any medium in a place that is always moist. A certain amount of moisture is needed, but it must be allowed to evaporate. Too little and the mushrooms will be brittle, dry, and have cracked caps. If this starts to happen, add some more moisture consistently. And the airflow is also a requirement, as a high level of CO^2 helps to prevent the 'fuzzy feet' mushrooms develop when there isn't enough fresh air.

Problem – Mushrooms Spoil Very Quickly After Harvesting

MUSHROOMS

If you harvest your mushrooms late, they can spoil. Don't harvest late or, if it cannot be avoided, use the mushrooms quickly. The best time to harvest is when the mushroom cap is dry and turned down. Try not to harvest when the mushrooms are wet.

If you are growing mushrooms for packaging and selling at a market, chill them before you package them and use breathable containers with cellophane covering.

You may come across other problems when you cultivate mushrooms, but these are the most likely ones. If you follow the steps carefully, you shouldn't run into any trouble. Make sure you do your research thoroughly before you start, making sure you use the correct medium and are growing in the right environment. Patience is key – time is a massive factor in mushroom cultivation> all you need to do is get things going, and then sit back and wait, monitoring your crop carefully of course.

BONUS CHAPTER

GROWING GOURMET MUSHROOMS FOR PROFIT – FAQ

Shiitake mushrooms, oysters, and other gourmet mushrooms are a joy to grow, especially if you have a decent market for selling them. Traditionally, they are grown outside on logs and can still be found in a lot of different areas. Now, though, you can grow them in bags indoors, using sawdust or straw as a growing medium.

Interested in making a pile of mushroom gold? These are the answers to the common questions about gourmet mushrooms:

1. Why would you consider gourmet mushrooms?

For two great reasons. First, when you grow them indoors, you can control the environment – the humidity, light, and temperature – to ensure you get the best possible crop. You get a bigger harvest, and that leads to more profit than you would get from traditional crops grown on logs. Second, you can get up to six crops every year from the same amount of space – more steady income.

2. Can gourmet mushrooms be grown in my area?

Because shiitake and oyster mushrooms will grow indoors, you can grow them whatever area you live in – you are not dependent on the outside climate. A shed will do the trick, a greenhouse, a barn even a spare room or basement can be used for growing.

3. Which mushrooms are the best?

Shiitake and oyster mushrooms are popular and easy to sell, simply because the market is already there. Stick with these, and you'll make your money. Yes, you could grow other exotics, but most need more skill than these two, and you might find it tougher to get your market.

4. How do you propagate gourmet mushrooms?

Because mushrooms belong to the fungi family, they produce spores, not seeds. Generally, the spores are cultivated on rye grain; when the grain has been 'colonized' by the growing plant, it is then used for inoculating the growing substrate or medium, usually sawdust from hardwood or straw. After inoculation, the mushrooms will spread, and we get the fruit – the mushrooms. Try it – it is a fantastic process to watch.

5. If I only grow mushrooms part-time, can I make any money?

Absolutely! Mushrooms don't take much space – a small area can produce large harvests. It is one of the best cash crops for people who don't have the land the time or even the inclination to grow large-scale, conventional crops. It only takes a couple of minutes every day to check on your bags of inoculated substrate. Most gourmet growers do it as a part-time job, working at their 'real' jobs the rest of the time.

6. Can I use compost to grow shiitake and oyster mushrooms?

You can, but it isn't the best medium, and it may cause issues leading to a smaller harvest. Most growers used sterilized substrates and grow indoors; that way, spores from wild mushrooms can't cause contamination. When your mushrooms have almost finished fruiting, and you chuck the substrate you used on the compost pile, you may get more, but it will only be a small yield.

7. When do I harvest the mushrooms?

Commercial growth of shiitake and oyster mushrooms is done indoors, where humidity, light, and temperature are controlled to ensure fast growth. When mushrooms appear, they come in what is known as 'flushes,' and you can expect the first one to be the largest – that's when it's time to bring in the first harvest. After that, there will be a few more flushes, but there won't be so many mushrooms – a lot f commercial growers tend to harvest only the first flush.

8. **Where can I sell gourmet mushrooms?**

The mushrooms are at their best when they are first picked, so most tend to be sold locally. Many growers sell to local restaurants, co-ops, foo stores and straight to customers at farmer's markets. Gourmet mushrooms don't ship to well, so its best to sell them fresh, locally. This also means you won't be competing with the commercial suppliers from out of state, and your customers know they are getting the freshest mushrooms.

9. **Can I make anything from the mushrooms?**

Yes. some of the most popular products are pickled mushrooms, dehydrated mushrooms, mushroom jerky (great for vegetarians), mushroom seasonings, and even your own growing kits.

10. **Do these mushrooms have better nutritional value than standard mushrooms?**

Studies show that shiitake and oyster mushrooms are high in nutrition and are medicinal in nature. They contain high levels of antioxidants to help protect your cells, of potassium, zinc, vitamin C, calcium, vitamin B, vitamin B2, and niacin. Shiitake mushrooms have also been shown to provide antiviral support, help lower cholesterol and support the cardiovascular system, as well as having immune-boosting properties and potential anticancer properties.

11. How much money can I make selling gourmet mushrooms?

The mushroom crop cycle is quite short, around six weeks, so in a small space, you can make a reasonably steady income. If you grow in bags indoors, you can produce around 25 pounds of mushrooms per square foot. Let's see what that translates to. We'll assume you are growing your mushrooms in a shed, 12 feet by 12 feet; that gives you a growing area of 144 square feet, and that could give you a yearly yield of 3600 pounds of mushrooms. Let's say the price is $12 per pound – half your crop is sold at that price and the rest at $6 per pound – that will get you a little more than $32,000 per year. Your expenses won't be too much – that's a pretty healthy income for a part-time job!

12. How much money do I need to start a business?

You don't need to splash out on tons of pricey equipment here, so the costs can be quite cheap, no more than a couple of hundred dollars. You will need the LED fluorescent lights, dirt cheap to buy and run, so your electricity bill won't even be noticeably affected – unless you are growing acres of mushrooms!

MUSHROOMS

By being able to grow these mushrooms inside, it doesn't matter where you are located and how much or little space you have available. You don't have to worry about the weather as you control the conditions, so really, the time is ripe for you to start your gourmet mushroom growing business now.

CONCLUSION

What more is there to say about mushrooms? Much, but for our purposes, we will conclude the book here. But there are a few things that I want to bring up before we end the book completely. There are many resources out there that will aid your experience with mushrooms, and many of these resources I have used throughout this book, so hopefully, these resources I give you will be of assistance to you in the near future:

Mushroom by Nicholas Money: This was a helpful resource for me when I was first starting out with my research. Nicholas discusses the overall political-ness of mushrooms and how they have changed the world as a whole, before moving on to more complex ideas I couldn't clearly comprehend. A good study for anyone with love for mushrooms.

Mushroom: A Global History by Cynthia Bertelsen: This was a terrific book, and the thoughts of Cynthia inspired much of the information found in this book. She clearly lays out the idea of mycophobia and mycophilia, namely the fear of mushrooms and the love of mushrooms. She is a wonderfully credible source, and I am glad to have found her early on in my research for this book, as she has led me through many discussions and interviews with friends and families on the subject of mushrooms. This is a wonderful introduction to mushrooms for anyone interested. A quick and easy read packed full of information

Alfie Aesthetics: No discussion of mushrooms is complete without talking about this semi-professional forager and mushroom hunter. He has a wonderful YouTube channel of 287K subscribers (his content deserves thousands more) and has plenty of different videos talking about his adventures in the woods looking for different edible and useful mushrooms. He does a lot of different videos dedicated to survival and entertaining commentaries on his experiences in the woods, so whatever you are looking for, I would suggest Alfie. One comment suggested that he has the knowledge of a college professor, the identification skills of a mycologist, and the humor of a drunk pervert, and I have got to say that is Alfie to a T. If that sounds appealing to you, PLEASE check this guy out. I wouldn't have wanted to write this book without his knowledge and enthusiasm for mushrooms and other fungi.

ID books: This is one of the helpful books you can look into getting once you get more and more serious on foraging for mushrooms. There are hundreds of other books you can look into, just make sure to get one that you can use in your own country and is up to date with all the best information and research. This book specifically helped me with research for random facts about mushrooms that helped with the overall flow of the book, so for a helpful book on identification and helpful facts as well, I would recommend this one for sure.

You have heard of all the benefits of mushrooms and such, whether they be health benefits or otherwise, and I hope this has given you some direction in which you want to start trying out mushrooms more in the near future. Here, I will review the information placed throughout the book in a manner that will allow you to go back and reference the information you are looking for in a quick way.

MUSHROOM FACTS

Common mushrooms to grow: Maitake, Enoki, Oyster, Shiitake, Lions Mane, and Wine Cap.

One quick step you need to follow in order to grow a mushroom: get the right substrate and container, steam pasteurization, incubation, and harvest.

There are several parts of mushrooms: spores, stem, gill, mycelium, hypha, volva, and the cap.

The life cycle of a mushroom is as follows: Inoculation, Spore Germination, Mycelial Expansion, Hyphal Knot, Primordia Formation, Fruitbody Selection, Mature Fruitbody, and Spore Release.

There are many wild, edible mushrooms out there on the North American continent, and it would serve you well to take the time to learn how to ID them. These include but are not limited to: The Field Mushroom, Caesar Mushroom, Honey Mushroom, Wood Ears, Giant Puffballs, Common Chanterelle, Smooth Chanterelle, Black Trumpets, Brick Tops, Lobster Mushrooms, Pear-Shaped Puffballs, The Parasol, Oysters, and Cauliflower Mushrooms.

There are seven categories of mushrooms: Cultivated Mushrooms, Wild Mushrooms, Medical Mushrooms, Psychoactive Mushrooms, Edible Mushrooms,

MUSHROOMS

Poisonous Mushrooms, Useful Mushrooms (For Other Reasons)